Portugal 1808

Portugal 1808

Wellington's First Peninsular Campaign

Tim Saunders

Pen & Sword
MILITARY

First published in Great Britain in 2024 by
PEN & SWORD MILITARY
an imprint of Pen & Sword Books Ltd
Yorkshire – Philadelphia

ISBN 978-1-03610-438-2

Typeset by Concept, Huddersfield, West Yorkshire, HD4 5JL.
Printed and bound in England by CPI Group (UK) Ltd, Croydon, CR0 4YY.

Pen & Sword Books Ltd incorporates the imprints of Aviation, Atlas, Family
History, Fiction, Maritime, Military, Discovery, Politics, History, Archaeology,
Select, Wharncliffe Local History, Wharncliffe True Crime, Military Classics,
Wharncliffe Transport, Leo Cooper, The Praetorian Press, Remember When,
White Owl, Seaforth Publishing and Frontline Books.

For a complete list of Pen & Sword titles please contact
PEN & SWORD BOOKS LTD
47 Church Street, Barnsley, South Yorkshire, S70 2AS, England
E-mail: enquiries@pen-and-sword.co.uk
Website: www.pen-and-sword.co.uk
or
PEN & SWORD BOOKS
1950 Lawrence Rd, Havertown, PA 19083, USA
E-mail: uspen-and-sword@casematepublishers.com
Website: www.penandswordbooks.com

Contents

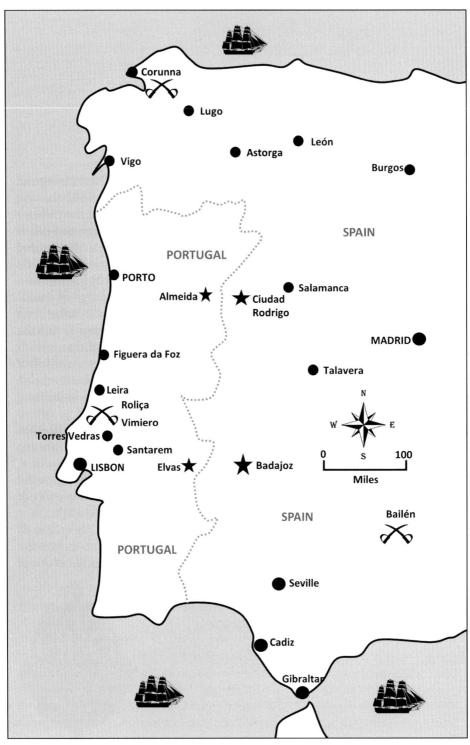

The western portion of the Iberian Peninsula.

Chapter One

The Peninsula 1807 and Early 1808

In 1806 in the aftermath of Jena and Auerstadt, Napoleon, 'master of Europe', issued the Berlin Decrees, instituting the Continental System, which closed the ports of Europe to British merchants. This, the emperor believed, would hit the 'nation of shopkeepers' and quickly cripple Britain's economy. The government in London, however, shunned all French offers of negotiation; remaining committed to doing everything they could to break Napoleonic supremacy in Europe. After Trafalgar there was no longer a serious threat of invasion, consequently, the British government turned to a policy described as 'filching sugar islands' from the French and Spanish as well as a peripheral strategy.[1]

Smuggling and evasion of the Continental System was commonplace, but both Sweden and Portugal at the extremities of Europe continued more or less discreetly to trade with British merchants. This was a threat and insult to Napoleon's authority, and something had to be done.

A month after the signing of the Treaty of Tilsit that marked the end of the short-lived Fourth Coalition, with Britain standing alone, on 12 August 1807 the French ambassador to Lisbon delivered an ultimatum from Napoleon to the Portuguese Prince Regent. This required him to declare war on Britain by 1 September, put his fleet of ten ships of the line at France's disposal, seize British goods in the country and arrest all British subjects.[2] Diplomatic relations with Britain were suspended, and ports were theoretically closed to British shipping, but the Prince Regent could not seize the wares of the Anglo-Portuguese merchants as this would have been economic suicide. His attempts to satisfy the emperor and to placate Britain did not, of course, satisfy Napoleon. Dealing with recalcitrant Portuguese traders and their government was, however, only one of his ambitions; he wanted to bring the whole of the Iberian Peninsula under his sway. In doing so he miscalculated and created his 'Spanish ulcer'.

Charles IV and Queen Maria Luisa sat on the Bourbon throne of Spain, being described respectively as 'imbecilic' and 'wicked'. Their 'duplicitous' son Prince Ferdinand was, however, the real power behind the throne along with his opponent the 'treacherous' Prime Minister Godoy, known as the Prince of Peace. In October 1807 they signed the first Treaty of Fontainebleau (a secret agreement with Napoleon), and in its codicils they agreed to

1

Napoleon, emperor of France, arguably the master of Europe in 1808.

permit a French corps to march through Spain to invade Portugal. In this conquest, Spanish armies would join the French and would split the country between them.[3]

Meanwhile, in south-west France the 25,000-strong Gironde Corps of Observation had assembled under General Junot and in mid-October began its march across Spain. In sixteen columns, the three infantry and one cavalry divisions made their way across northern Spain, a day's march apart in deteriorating weather conditions, reaching Salamanca in twenty-five days. Here they had expected a rest, but with the Royal Navy in the port of Lisbon they received orders to continue their march through the rain and crossed into Portugal in mid-November, largely ignorant of the geography of the country and the difficulties they would face.[4] The French were to find out that the terrain, which Wellesley appreciated had kept Portugal independent from Spain, despite its long frontier, made for difficult campaigning and was excellent defensive country. The Portuguese government was, however, in a state of disarray and, mesmerized by the approach of the French, did not mount a defence and declared war on Britain. Junot met the prime minister at Abrantes and according to General Foy he announced that: 'I shall be at Lisbon in four days,' and, said he, 'My soldiers are quite disconsolate that they have not fired a shot. Do not compel them to do it. I think you will be in the wrong if you do.'[5]

Having crossed into Portugal in mid-November with only the vaguest idea of the country's geography, along with a combination of bad weather and appalling roads, at the end of the month the leading handful of ragged French soldiers, with General Junot at their head, entered Lisbon looking nothing like:

> ... those formidable warriors before whom Europe was dumb and whose looks the [Portuguese] Prince Regent had not dared to encounter. A people possessed of a lively imagination had expected to see heroes of a superior species, colossuses, demigods ... A forced march of eighteen days, famine, torrents, inundated valleys and beating rain had debilitated their bodies and destroyed their clothing. They had hardly strength enough left to keep the step to the sound of the drum. A long file of lean, limping and mostly beardless soldiers followed with lagging pace the scantily filled masses of the battalions ... For the purposes of attack and defence, the troops had nothing but rusted firelocks and cartridges imbued with water. The Portuguese had been prepared to feel terror; the only feeling which they now experienced was that of vexation at having been astounded and brought under the yoke by a handful of foreigners.[6]

Junot's advance guard had arrived in Lisbon just in time to see the ships of the Portuguese navy with a fair wind bearing the Prince Regent, much of the nobility and half the nation's money slipping away from the rock of Lisbon, out into the Atlantic. With Admiral Sir Sidney Smith and six first-class sail of the Royal Navy as an escort, they were bound for the Portuguese colony of Brazil.

Realizing his precarious situation, Junot attempted to rule the city with a light hand (for a French general), attempting to calm the worst fears of the population of Lisbon by trying to keep his soldiers on a tight rein and doing his best to prevent looting. Napoleon, however, undermined these attempts with orders to seize the property of the estimated 15,000 people, including 300 Anglo-Portuguese families that had fled the country and to levy a

The flight of the Portuguese court and Royal Family.

100-million franc fine on the treasury. The country was, however, bereft of specie, with the aristocracy and merchants having emptied the banks and carried off their portable wealth. Junot was only just able gather sufficient money and goods with which to supply his army. These taxes and requisitions were deeply resented by the population and, with an increasingly onerous occupation and the executions of citizens who refused to hand over money and possessions to the French, the situation across the country was becoming ripe for revolution. The majority of Portugal's natural leadership had, however, abandoned their estates, creating a vacuum with no one of stature to lead a nascent insurrection.

French Usurpation of Spain and the Dos de Mayo Revolt

During the autumn of 1807, with attention firmly focused on the fate of Portugal, Napoleon was assembling a second, much larger force. This was not the 40,000-strong corps stipulated in the Treaty of Fontainebleau 'in case Britain should threaten an armed descent on Portugal', but a 75,000-strong army. Commanded by Prince Murat, this force stealthily entered Spain and secured strategic points, while Charles IV and his son Ferdinand were lured to Bayonne on the pretext of mediating between them. Charles was forced to abdicate and Ferdinand VII took the Spanish throne as a French puppet, but this arrangement did not last long. Feelings against the French were running high and open rebellion broke out in Madrid. However, Murat's brutal suppression of the Dos de Mayo Revolt only fanned the flames of what had up to this point been largely nascent rebellions across Spain. Fractious provincial juntas took control of their regions and began raising troops and Napoleon was forced to send another 20,000 men to reinforce his army and hold down the rebellious country.[7] Dupont's defeat at Bailén and a reverse at Zaragoza were only the headline events amid what was for the French a rapidly deteriorating situation.

While he was fighting the Austrians in a campaign in the Danube Valley during August 1808, Napoleon placed his elder brother Joseph on the Spanish throne. Sending him to Madrid from the Kingdom of Naples where he was a successful popular ruler was not what Joseph wanted. In Spain, Joseph was immediately dammed by his Spanish opponents, who referred to him as *Pepe Botella* ('Joe Bottle') at every opportunity, alleging he drank heavily, despite his well-known moderation! Placing Joseph, the usurper, on the throne of Spain, along with Napoleonic France's new institutions, laws and philosophy only served to widened the rebellion against French rule.

Joseph Bonaparte, King of Spain.

In his invasion and by luring King Charles IV and forcing him to abdicate in favour of Ferdinand VII and subsequently replacing him with Joseph, Napoleon had yet again overreached himself. He had wrongly believed that the removal of the unpopular and venal Bourbons, along with their corrupt government, would be popular with the Spanish population. On top of that, with Murat's actions in the resulting Dos de Mayo Revolt, Napoleon created the beginnings of his 'Spanish ulcer', which in the summer of 1808 alone resulted in the loss of almost 40,000 men. Over the following six years the war in the Peninsula was a crippling haemorrhage of French military power.

Back in Portugal, following the brutal suppression of the Dos de Mayo and the consequent revolt that spread across Spain, General Junot and his army found that their lines of communication back to France were cut by Spanish armies and bands of guerrillas. The last message he received in Lisbon from Napoleon during May ordered him to detach 4,000 of his 25,000 men to Marshal Bessières at Ciudad Rodrigo. When news of events in Madrid reached Oporto on 6 June the Spanish division that provided the garrison abandoned the French and marched back to Spain to confront its erstwhile ally and within days, the north of Portugal joined Spain in open revolt against

Prince Murat's brutal suppression of the Dos de Mayo Rebellion by Goya. The inclusion of French Mameluke cavalrymen is a political reference going back to the Muslim conquest of Spain.

the French occupation. Meanwhile, Spanish envoys were dispatched to London from the country's Northern Province, the Asturias, to request money and arms to further what was becoming a general uprising.

Britain Changes Course

At the beginning of 1808 there seemed little prospect of the British army being able to return to the mainland of central Europe to take on the French. Recent military expeditions to the Low Countries and garrisoning King George's Hanover had failed in the face of the strength of French revolutionary and Napoleonic armies. Short campaigns around the edges of the Continent had, however, been more successful. In pursuance of the peripheral strategy, in May 1808 Lieutenant General Sir John Moore had sailed with a force of 10,000 men to the Baltic where he was to support Gustavus IV of Sweden, whose country was threatened by France and its then allies Russia, and Denmark. Sir John's fleet arrived off Sweden on 17 May, but he was not permitted to land his troops at Gothenburg; however, he was summoned to Stockholm to confer with Gustavus. The king proposed 'crazy schemes of conquest' in which he suggested that the British and Swedes should jointly seize Zealand and attack Russian-held Finland. The British general expressed his strongest doubts and an angry Gustavus ordered Sir John to remain in the capital, but Moore made his escape to Gothenburg dressed as a peasant and sailed with his troops back to England. Full of resentment and embarrassment, Sir John believed he had been sent on a fool's errand for Westminster's own party-political reasons and wrote that 'the service was the most painful on which I have been employed.'

In execution of the other British strategy, the 'filching of sugar islands', despite the disaster at Buenos Aires the previous year a 9,000-man-strong expedition was being prepared in Cork under Lieutenant General Sir Arthur Wellesley. The objective was to support a rebellion in the Spanish colony of Venezuela. A third expedition of 5,000 men under General Spencer was assembling in Gibraltar with a view to operations in the Mediterranean.

The news that the Spanish envoys bore of events in their country had the British government promptly reconsidering their plans for the remainder of 1808. The newly-promoted Lieutenant General Sir Arthur Wellesley, MP and member of the government, stated in a memorandum summarizing his view that now was the time to commit to the Peninsula 'all the disposable force that can immediately be spared from England ... to be prepared to act as circumstances would point out':

> The events which have lately occurred in Spain, and the intelligence received from Gibraltar, appear to deserve the serious attention of the King's Ministers. There can be no doubt that the events which preceded

the massacre at Madrid, and the revolution effected at Bayonne, had excited the jealousy of the whole Spanish nation; and the late outrages have induced some persons high in authority and command in Spain to manifest a disposition to resist the execution of the plans for the subjugation of their country.

Indeed Bonaparte himself does not appear to consider the situation of his affairs in Spain to be very prosperous; he has remarked upon the sentiments and proceedings of some of the Spaniards; and we find that he has called large reinforcements to the assistance of his troops.

Upon the whole then this would appear to be a crisis in which a great effort might be made with advantage; and it is certain that any measures which can distress the French in Spain must oblige them to delay for a season the execution of their plans upon Turkey, or to withdraw their armies from the north.[8]

Lord Canning, the Foreign Secretary, summed up the view of the government when he spoke in Parliament in mid-June:

His Majesty's Ministers see with as deep and lively an interest … the noble struggle which the Spanish nation are now making to resist the unexampled atrocity of France and preserve the independence of their country; and there exists the strongest disposition on the part of the British Government to afford every practicable aid in a contest so magnanimous. In endeavouring to afford this aid, it will never occur to us to consider that a state of war exists between this country and Spain. Whenever any nation in Europe starts up with a determination to oppose a power which, whether professing insidious peace or declaring open war, is alike the common enemy of all other people, that nation, whatever its former relation may be, becomes, *ipso facto*, the ally of Great Britain.[9]

Unusually there was unanimity between the Tory government and the Whig opposition, who usually protested about aiding 'effete despotisms of the continent'. Prime Minister Portland's Cabinet decided to cancel its orders for the expedition to Venezuela, preferring to assist the rebellions in the Iberian Peninsula. With Spain and Britain having been until very recently these long-standing enemies it was a clear case of 'my enemy's enemy is my friend'.

Having resolved in remarkably quick time to mount a force for service in the Peninsula, even though the campaigning season was well advanced, Lieutenant General Wellesley received fresh orders from the commander-in-chief, the Duke of York:

Sir,   Horse Guards, 14th June, 1808.
His Majesty having been graciously pleased to appoint you to the command of a detachment of his army, to be employed on a particular

Frederick, Duke of York, the Commander-in-Chief in 1808.

service, I have to desire that you will be pleased to take the earliest opportunity to assume command of this force and carry into effect such instructions you may receive from his Majesty's ministers.[10] [See Appendix I for a full transcript of Sir Arthur's orders.]

Assembly of the Expedition

Even though Wellesley's 7,000 men in Southern Ireland and General Spencer's 3,000 men from Gibraltar had been warned for their respective operations, preparations were far from complete and further complicated by the change of objective and the prospect of fighting the French rather than supporting rebels. Consequently, in three weeks Wellesley had to overcome sundry administrative and logistic difficulties, while navigating the labyrinthine structure of the Georgian army. These included officers and drivers of the Irish Wagon Train, whose horses were to be allocated to the artillery, not being required to serve outside Ireland and releasing camp equipage from the

Treasury-controlled Ordnance Board, plus transporting it to Ireland. The latter included such basic items as soldiers' water canteens and haversacks. Also under the Ordnance Board were the various commissaries, most of whom it transpired had very little idea of the execution of their duties in the field.

The frustration Wellesley experienced at Cork is evident in a note to Lord Castlereagh, the Secretary of State for War and the Colonies:

> I declare that I do not understand the principles on which our military establishments are formed, if, when large corps are sent out to perform important and difficult service, they are not to have with them those means of equipment they require, such as horses to draw artillery, and drivers attached to the commissariat.

The sundry delays added up, which meant that, for instance, the four companies of the 2nd Battalion 95th Rifles having sailed from Dover had to wait aboard ship in Cork Cove for five weeks. Wellesley gave orders that the troops so confined be either taken ashore daily for drill and exercise or where possible transferred to barrack accommodation ashore. Despite these measures, the troops would invariably lose condition during a protracted period of confinement.

Captain William Warre described the wait in a letter to his mother:

> It is very uncertain when we shall sail. We are waiting for the *Donegal* 74 [guns], Captain Malcolm, and *Crocodile* frigate, and for some transports, with artillery and cavalry, and some empty ones to thin those now here, which are much overcrowded, though hitherto quite healthy. The additional room allowed looks like a longer voyage than expected, though cavalry and our taking horses seems to contradict this idea.

Wellesley's detailed orders, issued by the government on 30 June, were based on information received from the Spanish envoys, which proved to be largely inaccurate. They significantly underestimated the number of French soldiers in the various enemy armies in Spain and Portugal and were hopelessly over-optimistic about their ability to defeat the French occupier. On that basis they had been instructed to specifically discourage the offer of sending British troops to Spain. Instead, they were to suggest a deployment to Portugal, which would tie down Junot's army and protect the Spanish armies from attack from that quarter.

Sailing from Cork was delayed by the necessity of waiting for 394 men of the 20th Light Dragoons, not all with horses, to arrive from Portsmouth and then by contrary winds. The fleet bearing the expedition eventually sailed on 12 July to what was for most an unknown destination. Rifleman Harris wrote

Viscount Castlereagh, Secretary of State for War. His attempts to manipulate army seniority, court influence and politics to install a 'puppet commander' failed.

that 'our sails were given the wind, and amidst cheers of our comrades we sailed majestically out of the Cove of Cork for the hostile shore.'

A good passage to the rendezvous off Cape Finisterre could be expected to take the transports anything from five to twenty-one days depending on seasonal winds and weather.

A Change of Command

With the fleet having sailed for the Peninsula, only days later the government decided to increase the size of the force; first of all with the troops assembling at Ramsgate and Harwich under Brigadiers Acland and Anstruther. These two brigades of infantry had been preparing to raid the by now virtually undefended port of Boulogne, with the objective of destroying the part of the French fleet lying there inactive. Secondly, with Sir John Moore's 10,000-strong expedition, whose return from the Baltic was imminent. Once fully deployed during the autumn this would eventually produce an army with an effective strength of just under 30,000 men, but the force that landed in the Peninsula in the opening days of the war was just 15,000 strong.

Lieutenant General Wellesley had sailed from Cork unaware that with the increase in scale of the commitment, questions were now being raised regarding his leadership of the Peninsular expedition. While Canning, a political ally of Sir Arthur, was happy to vest command in him, he was, however, the army's junior lieutenant general, having been promoted as recently as 25 April 1808. Not only was Wellesley's position questioned due to his lack of seniority and the force being considered to be a more senior officer's command, there were also political dimensions and matters of individuals' patronage at Court and in Horse Guards at play.

Sir John Moore was not only senior to Wellesley, he was also an accomplished general and would in that respect have been the natural choice. He was, however, unpopular with the politicians as he spoke his mind and was abrasive in his dealings with them. Consequently, the government would not give Moore command. Instead, they placed General Sir Hew Dalrymple, who as Governor of Gibraltar was well versed in the situation in Spain, in 'temporary command'. Fortesque theorizes that it was intended that command would eventually devolve on Wellesley.[11] A section of Castlereagh's letter to Dalrymple certainly points in this direction: 'Permit me to recommend to your particular confidence Lieut. General Sir Arthur Wellesley. His high reputation in the service as an officer would in itself dispose you, I am persuaded, to select him for any service that required great prudence and temper, combined with much military experience.'[12]

Dalrymple's second-in-command, General Sir Harry Burrard, was appointed thanks to the influence of the Duke of York. This additional layer of command was a transparent measure to prevent the expedition devolving on Sir John Moore once Dalrymple returned to Gibraltar. It is widely believed that Moore's whole treatment was designed to induce him to resign when he heard that two indifferent officers had been placed in command above him.

The following letter from Castlereagh eventually caught up with Wellesley while at sea:

> I am to acquaint you that his Majesty has been pleased to intrust the command of his troops serving on the coasts of Spain and Portugal to Lieut. General Sir Hew Dalrymple, with Lieut. General Sir Harry Burrard, second in command.
>
> The Lieut. General has been furnished with copies your instructions up to the present date exclusive. These instructions you will be pleased to carry into execution with every expedition that circumstances will

permit, without awaiting the arrival of the Lieut. General, reporting to him your proceedings. And should you be previously joined by a senior officer, you will in that case communicate to him your orders and afford him every assistance in carrying them into execution.

It would take some time for Burrard to reach the Peninsula from the UK and for a message to reach Gibraltar, then for Dalrymple to sail north from Gibraltar to take command. In the meantime, Wellesley would remain in command and direct operations.

In accordance with his orders, Wellesley arrived off A Coruña on 20 July, having made good speed aboard the frigate HMS *Crocodile*. In conversation with the Galician Junta he was told that virtually the whole country was in arms against the French and that despite being routed at Medina de Rioseco on 14 July, other Spanish armies had defeated enemy detachments. Wellesley, however, stressed in a note to Lord Castlereagh that this was all from unofficial sources and likely to be hopelessly over-optimistic. General Dupont had, by the time of Wellesley's visit to A Coruña, been defeated at Bailén, but news was unlikely to have reached north-west.

The Junta reiterated their request for arms and money and continued to suggest that assistance to Portugal, which was in a state of rebellion, was the best course of action for the British, who should sail south to Oporto. This Sir Arthur did, making a speedy five-day passage.

Arriving off the mouth of the Duero, Wellesley found the mood of the Portuguese Junta headed by the Bishop of Oporto in a very different frame of mind, having given up any hope of help from the Spanish, which until Medina de Rioseco had seemed likely. In these circumstances the Portuguese were

Assembly of Wellesley's division in Cork and follow-on forces.

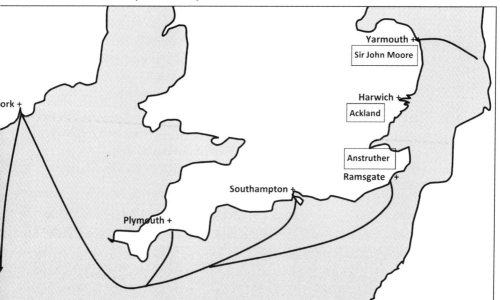

The British Peninsular Army of 1808

Wellesley's forces consisted of the following:

	Infantry	Cavalry	Artillery
(1) Division embarked at Cork:			
20th Light Dragoons (only 180 with horses)		394	
Artillery			226
5th Regiment (1st batt.)	990		
9th Regiment (1st batt.)	833		
36th Regiment	591		
38th Regiment (1st batt.)	957		
40th Regiment (1st batt.)	926		
45th Regiment (1st batt.)	670		
60th Rifles (5th batt.)	936		
71st Regiment (1st batt.)	903		
91st Regiment (1st batt.)	917		
95th Rifles (2nd batt., four companies)	400		
	8,123		
(2) Spencer's troops from Andalusia:			
Artillery			245
6th Regiment (1st batt.)	946		
29th Regiment	806		
32nd Regiment (1st batt.)	874		
50th Regiment (1st batt.)	948		
82nd Regiment (1st batt.)	929		
	4,503	394	471

A total of 12,626 infantry, 394 cavalry, 471 artillery = 13,491[1]

In addition, there were troops en route to the Peninsula including Acland's and Anstruther's brigades that were still embarking as at 20 July 1808:

(3) Anstruther's Brigade from Ramsgate consisted of:	
9th Regiment (2nd batt.)	633
43rd Regiment (2nd batt.)	721
52nd Regiment (2nd batt.)	654
97th Regiment	695
	2,703
(4) Of Acland's Brigade from Harwich there were:	
2nd or Queen's Regiment	731
20th Regiment (seven and a half companies)	401
95th Rifles (1st batt., two companies)	200
	1,332

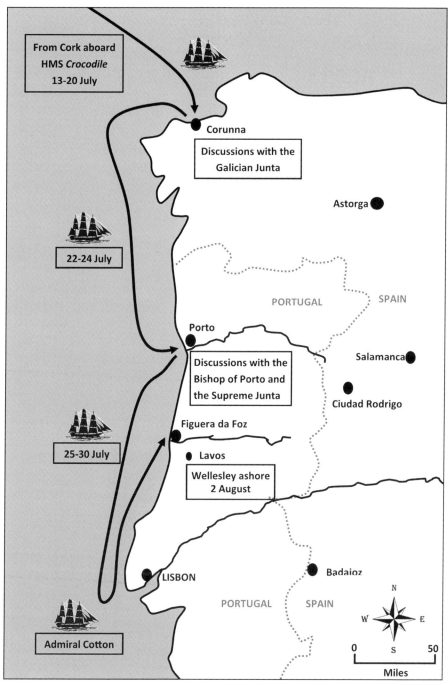

Wellesley's movements prior to landing at Mondego Bay.

more than amenable to accepting British help as their ability to fight the French with any prospect of winning was virtually non-existent. Taking on General Junot and liberating Lisbon and therefore Portugal was the joint aim.

The Junta recommended disembarking approximately 65 miles further south at the mouth of the Rio Mondego, where there was a landing-place that offered some shelter from the Atlantic rollers. Other points in favour of Mondego Bay were that Fort Figueira,[13] at the mouth of the river, was already garrisoned by 300 Royal Marines and with a reduced distance of 100 miles from Lisbon it was a logistically sustainable option.[14]

António de São José de Castro, Bishop of Oporto, was an important figure in welcoming British intervention in the Peninsular.

Chapter Two

The 1808 Campaign Begins

The fleet arrived off the mouth of the Rio Mondego at Figueira da Foz on 30 July and having spent two days hiring local boats with which to supplement those of the Royal Navy, General Wellesley's 10,000 men began to disembark on 1 August.[1] Despite being told of the shelter offered by the mouth of the Mondego, there was no such protection from the Atlantic rollers for the anchored ships. A sandbar across the mouth of the estuary meant that the maximum draft of craft that could get into the shelter of the river was just 11 feet. Captain Leach of the 95th Rifles recalled the discomfort:

> About the second week in July the expedition sailed, and at the expiration of a fortnight we were off the coast of Portugal, near Oporto, whence we steered to Mondego Bay and anchored. Although the weather was perfectly calm, I never remember to have experienced more motion in a gale of wind, than we felt during the six days spent at this anchorage. The long and heavy swell made the yards of the ship at times almost touch the water, as she rolled from side to side, which caused some awful breakages amongst our wine glasses and crockery-ware.[2]

First to be transferred into boats and rowed ashore were Major Robert Travers' four companies of 2nd 95th and several of the 5th 60th Rifles, followed by the 45th Foot, all of Fane's brigade.[3] Clambering from the rolling hulls of the transports into the tossing boats was difficult enough, but as Leach observed 'the process of passing the bar of sand, on which there is, even in the finest weather, a dangerous surf running, was affected, I believe, without anything more serious than some wet jackets.' Leach records that once ashore:

> Whilst we were drawing up our men near the landing-place, and waiting for further orders, we were beset with a host of padres, friars and monks, of all ages, each carrying a huge umbrella of the most gaudy colour imaginable; intended, no doubt, to protect their complexions, which vied with those of chimney sweeps. These gentry welcomed us with *vivas*, and protested that, with our assistance, every Frenchman in Portugal should speedily be annihilated. Our visitors were not confined to the

Major Robert Travers commanded the wing of four companies of the 2nd Battalion, 95th Rifles.

male sex; for some olive beauties, with sparkling eyes and jet black hair, were induced to take a peep at us; and, before we parted, some of the more favoured of us were presented with flowers and fruit from the hands of these damsels.

Brigadier General Fane's task for his 6th or Light Brigade was to advance some 2 miles south-east to the village of Lavos where he was to deploy piquets and patrols to cover the beachhead and the disembarkation. Rifleman Harris recorded:

We were immediately pushed forward up country in advance of the main body. The climate was hot, with a burning sun above our heads, and our feet sinking at every step into the hot sand, and we soon began to feel the misery of the frightful load we were condemned to march and fight under.[4]

While for much of this first peninsular campaign the soldiers were indeed very heavily laden, Harris's memory on this occasion fails him. The soldiers landed with a haversack containing three days' cooked food and a blanket or greatcoat suspended by a blanket strap, with necessities rolled therein. The heavily packed soldiers' knapsacks remained on board the ships for the time being.

Captain Patterson of the 50th Foot, having been flung out of a boat into the surf for a wet landing, details what was carried on his battalion's march to Lavos:

> After this delightful immersion, and the cold reception we had experienced, on our first appearance upon the Lusitanian stage, we moved forward, with habiliments of war effectually saturated by the briny element, and soon joined our *companions of the bath*, already on the road. Most of us had been provided with small knapsacks, holding our *kit*, together with the haversack, and canteen, slung across the shoulder; of which the two former (including their contents), were rendered totally unfit for service, nothing being left for consolation but the brandy, or rum; cordials which were well calculated, and by no means unnecessary, to elevate our drooping spirits.[5]

Captain William Warre, an ADC in 2nd Brigade that came ashore 2 August, describes the routine in the village of Lavos during the disembarkation:

> General Ferguson's staff here occupy an old fellow's house, where we are comfortable enough, from Mrs Wm. Archer of Figueira's attention in sending us out everything we can want. Otherwise, I know not what we should have done, as Figueira is 4½ miles off, and not a thing eatable or drinkable (besides the rations) nearer. We are up in the morning at 3 a.m., and, what with visiting the outposts, or line, and guards, 7 or 8 hours a day on horse or mule back, so that we are quite ready to lie down 3 in a small room (for which luxury we are not a little envied), at nine o'clock, and sleep as sound as on the finest down beds in the world, but for turning out now and then in the night, to interpret or some other trifle (from nobody speaking the language but me in the brigade), which now consists of the 66th, 40th, 71st Highlanders, all tried regiments on service, and longing to meet these so much vaunted Frenchmen.[6]

Also during the disembarkation, Sir Arthur wrote to the Duke of Richmond in Ireland from HMS *Donegal*, to which he had transferred for comfort and to

A rifleman in light marching order. In addition to his leather accoutrements he is carrying a haversack for rations, a water canteen and a blanket strap with, in this case, a greatcoat.

be alongside Captain Malcolm. In this letter he updated the duke on his plans once General Spencer's force had arrived and gave a remarkably muted reaction to news that he was to be superseded in command:[7]

> I shall commence my operations as soon as he [Spencer] with his 5,000, or a reinforcement expected from England of 5,000 men, shall join me. He sent this same account to England, where they took the alarm, and ordered out 5,000 men and Moore's corps of 10,000 men, with several general officers, senior to me, and Sir Hew Dalrymple to command the whole army. I hope that I shall have beat Junot before any of them shall arrive, and then they will do as they please with me. I think it possible, however, that the ministry may wish me to return to you.[8]

Meanwhile, the process of getting the army ashore continued. Sergeant Landscheit, who was serving in one of the two squadrons of the 20th Light Dragoons, recalled the landing with horses:

> The shores of Mondego Bay are open and shelving, so as to produce, when the winds blow fresh, a heavy surf; and it so happened that we brought with us to our anchorage just enough of a breeze to render the task of disembarkation a difficult one. Several boats were upset, and out of the infantry corps which landed first, some men were lost, though I believe that the casualties were not numerous. But for us, we suffered nothing. We were directed to stand upright in the boats, with bridle in hand, and prepared, in case of any accident, to spring into the saddle; a judicious precaution, which proved in two or three instances eminently useful. One punt capsized upon the surf; but no lives were lost, because the horses, sometimes swimming, sometimes wading, carried their riders ashore. We then formed upon the beach, and carrying each man his three days' provisions, ready cooked, pushed forward to a village, the name of which I have forgotten, and there took up our quarters.[9,10]

Captain Ross-Lewin of the 32nd arriving with Spencer's force described the landing and, after several boats being upset, saw how it was possible to get ashore:

> At length it was observed that a certain rock broke off the surf in some measure, and it was thought that the troops might be landed inside it from the flat-bottomed boats.
> As many as the boats could safely carry were then ordered into them, and they pulled off in succession to the rock. The Portuguese on this part of the coast were very zealous, and, being expert swimmers, rendered great service during the whole operation. They swam about the boats, diving under the heavier waves, and reappearing in the hollow of the sea,

The British landing-place on the southern side of the Rio Mondego opposite Figueira da Foz.

ready to pick up any soldiers whose boats might be swamped. According as the flat boats reached the rock, the Portuguese placed our men across their shoulders, and carried them, their arms, ammunition and three days' provisions, in perfect safety to the shore. No people could have behaved better, and very few would have behaved so well; they were full of enthusiasm; they regarded us their future deliverers from the insolence and oppression of the French, and they certainly adopted a handsome method of giving us a welcome to their land.[11]

As Wellesley had feared when he wrote to Lord Castlereagh from Cork, on arrival in Portugal he found a paucity of means to mount and move his army. The Junta had undertaken to provide these but only delivered about sixty horses, which brought the 20th Hussars to a total of 240 mounted men. In addition, sufficient mules and horses were collected to, alongside the Irish Commissariat horses, draw three batteries of guns and caissons. The guns to march with the army totalled five 9-pounders, ten 6-pounders and three howitzers. Similarly, there were insufficient mules and carts for supplies. A total of 500 mules were procured through the Junta and locally by purchase, but 300 bullock carts had to be requisitioned. This was sufficient to carry the reserve of artillery ammunition and thirteen days of rations but not to draw General Spencer's two batteries, which had to be left behind.

In all it took five days to land Wellesley's force and a further three days were required to land Spencer's troops, guns and stores from Gibraltar, bringing the army up to a strength of 15,000 men. Ensign Leslie arrived off

Very basic local bullock carts were used where possible.

Figueira da Foz with the 29th Foot, a part of Spencer's force from Cádiz on 6 August:

> There we received orders to disembark next morning. All was now bustle on board. Animation shone in every countenance. Everyone was employed in selecting a few articles requisite for campaign, and getting their heavy baggage secured. This was effected with small trouble. A tremendous swell caused the ship to roll in the most violent manner, and everything was slipping and flying about.

After a difficult crossing of the sandbar, it was not until evening that the 29th Foot marched to Lavos:

> It was late when we reached the army's encampment on the heights above the small town of Lavos. It was so dark that we had some difficulty in finding our tents; and in regard to food nothing whatever could be got, so we contented ourselves with a morsel of ships' biscuits and a glass of rum from our haversacks. We then wrapped ourselves in our cloaks, and lay down on the *benty* grass, eagerly seeking repose after our fatigues.

Plan and Co-Operation with the Portuguese

In 1807 General Junot on his arrival in Lisbon had disbanded most of the Portuguese army and shipped off the best to Germany. The country's army of 1808 was born out of the rebellion against the French, but it was not

By the Commanders in Chief of His Britannic Majesty's Land and Sea Forces, employed to assist the loyal Inhabitants of the Kingdom of Portugal,

'PEOPLE OF PORTUGAL,

'The time is arrived to rescue your country, and restore the government of your lawful Prince.

'His Britannic Majesty, our most gracious King and master, has, in compliance with the wishes and ardent supplications for succour from all parts of Portugal, sent to your aid a British army, directed to co-operate with his fleet, already on your coast.

'The English soldiers, who land upon your shore, do so with every sentiment of friendship, faith, and honor.

'The glorious struggle in which you are engaged is for all that is dear to man, the protection of your wives and children, the restoration of your lawful prince, the independence, nay, the very existence of your kingdom, and for the preservation of your holy religion; objects like these can only be obtained by distinguished examples of fortitude and constancy.

'The noble struggle against the tyranny and usurpation of France, will be jointly maintained by Portugal, Spain, and England; and in contributing to the success of a cause so just and glorious, the views of his Britannic Majesty are the same as those by which you are yourselves animated.

'ARTHUR WELLESLEY.

'Lavaos, 2nd Aug., 1808.'   'CHARLES COTTON.

Wellesley's proclamation to the Portuguese population.

well-founded. Captain Warre, himself Anglo-Portuguese, described the state of this army in a letter home: 'The Portuguese have about 28,000 men in all the kingdom, in arms of all descriptions, all badly armed, and I fear not so enthusiastic in the cause (though they boast much) as their neighbours the Spaniards.'

On his arrival at Oporto Wellesley had spoken to Colonel Browne, who was already distributing support to the Portuguese and what he told him cannot have filled him with confidence. From his reports it appeared that there were:

no Spanish troops in the north of Portugal, and that all the Portuguese force was upon the Mondego, to the south of which river the insurrection had already spread. A French division of 8,000 men was supposed to be in their front, and some great disaster was to be expected, for ... with every good will in the people, their exertions were so short-lived, and with so little combination, that there was no hope of their being able to resist the advances of the enemy.[12]

Of the Portuguese army in the field north of the Mondego, Browne reported that it consisted of 5,000 regular soldiers and militia that were 'half armed' and some 12,000 unarmed peasants. While the disembarkation was under way Wellesley crossed the river and rode 10 miles inland to Montemor-o-Velho to meet the Portuguese commander *Marechal de Campo* Bernardim Freire de Andrade, who proposed a joint campaign in the interior of the country. This Wellesley rejected, 'having already discovered the weakness of the insurrection' and not believing the promise of 'ample stores of provisions', but he

Commander of the Portuguese army General Bernardim Freire de Andrade.

placated his ally with 5,000 muskets and accoutrements. Freire reluctantly agreed, but pressed Wellesley to advance on Leiria where there was a French stores magazine.

General Wellesley's campaign plan was to advance the 100 miles south to Lisbon, which was politically and militarily the heart and soul of Portugal. He and his Portuguese allies would do so by routes within 10 miles of the coast, marching via Leiria, Alcobaça and Torres Vedras rather than Santarém and the Tagus Valley. This course of action was dictated by the army's need to be supplied by the ships of the Royal Navy, as the country could not supply the necessary flour for bread. It was also necessary for the army to protect the landing of the reinforcements, namely Anstruther's and Acland's brigades at Maceira Bay. Wellesley explained to the Cintra Inquiry that there were also wider reasons:

> If I had adopted the line by the high road from Lisbon to the north by Santarém, I must have kept up my communication with the Mondego; which would have weakened my force for operations in the field, and after all, the enemy with his cavalry must have broken in upon it. By adopting the line by the sea coast, and depending for my supplies upon the shipping, my communication was so short that it defended itself; I was enabled to keep my force collected in one body, and I had my arsenals and magazines close to me whenever required to communicate with them.[13]

Wellesley wrote to General Burrard suggesting that when General Moore's division arrived it should land at Figueira da Foz and march south-east from the Mondego to Santarém on the Tagus. This advance would firstly cover Wellesley's left flank, particularly from the threat of intervention by Marshal Bessières who was positioned around Ciudad Rodrigo and Almeida, and secondly cut off one of Junot's avenues of escape. (The text of Wellesley's note explaining his campaign plan to Admiral Cotton appears in Appendix II.)

The French Response

When word of the British landing at Figueira da Foz and its scale reached General Junot in Lisbon, his 26,000-strong corps was dispersed in garrisons as far east as Elvas and Almeida or 'pacifying the country and levying contributions'. General Loison with his division of 7,000 men was, for instance, in the east of Portugal, where he brutally suppressed a rebellious stand on 30 July at Évora. After the fighting his troops massacred prisoners and the entire population, including women and children totalling some 2,000 souls. This act striking at the seat of the Junta of the Central Alentejo region was of course designed to be a warning to other increasingly rebellious provinces.

General Junot ordered the concentration of his corps' three divisions, which after deducting the aforementioned garrisons and those left in Lisbon, Wellesley calculated as numbering 14,000 men. This force was to march to confront the combined British and Portuguese, but they would take time to assemble. Consequently, on 6 August Junot dispatched General Delaborde with 2,500 men and a light artillery battery south to Alcobaça with orders to delay an Anglo-Portuguese advance south to Lisbon. On the 10th a regiment joined him at Alcobaça from Peniche, bringing his command to a strength of approximately 5,000 men, with which he advanced north to Batalha.

General Jean-Andoche Junot, commander of the French VIII Corps in Portugal.

Isolated from the other French armies in the Peninsula and faced with the prospect of overwhelming enemy numbers, Junot could have been forgiven for considering abandoning Portugal and withdrawing to Spain. General Foy, however, explains that:

> Though the Emperor had not given any positive orders on this subject, either before or since the disturbances in Spain, the General looked upon himself as responsible to him for holding the country. Had any one proposed to evacuate Portugal, while there existed the slightest probability of reaching the Ebro without sustaining a considerable loss, the proposal would have been scouted by the unanimous feeling of the army. Preparations were made to march against the enemy, for the purpose of giving battle.[14]

Junot eventually marched from Lisbon on 15 August and rendezvoused with Loison on the 17th at Cercal.

General Wellesley had been concerned about a potential threat to his flank from the hesitant Marshal Bessières who was positioned around Ciudad Rodrigo and Almeida, but with news that King Joseph had abandoned Madrid, Sir Arthur could safely march without waiting for Sir John Moore. He was now confident that the threat posed by the isolated Bessières was much reduced, as the marshal had his own lines of communication to protect, let alone an advance into Portugal.

Orders for the March

From the outset, with tales of French depredations and just how much that behaviour served to turn the Portuguese population against them, Wellesley issued a reminder to his army that they were campaigning in a friendly country. In a substantial General Order covering logistics and administration, he wrote:

> The officers and soldiers are to understand that they are to pay for everything they require from the country, excepting provisions, forage, wood and carriages allowed by the public. For these articles when required, and not issued by the Commissary, they will make requisitions in the country, and give receipts; but they are to make these requisitions only by order of a General or other officer commanding a brigade or detachment: and in case any officer should pass his receipt for any article for which he ought to pay, or should sign a receipt for which he may not be authorized by the officer commanding the brigade or detachment to which he belongs, the Commissary will receive directions to charge such articles to the officer who shall have given the receipt, and such officer will also be liable to the penalties of disobedience of orders.[15]

In preparation for the march on Lisbon, General Wellesley reorganized his army into six brigades, four consisting of three battalions and two of two battalions:

1st Brigade	General Hill	1/5th, 1/9th, 1/38th
2nd Brigade	General Ferguson	1/36th, 1/40th, 1/71st
3rd Brigade	General Nightingall	1/29th, 1/82nd
4th Brigade	General Bowes	1/6th, 1/32nd
5th Brigade	General C. Craufurd	1/45th, 1/50th, 1/91st
6th (Light) Brigade	General Fane	5/60th Rifles
		4 coys 2/95th Rifles

At 0300 hours on 9 August, a day ahead of the main force, Fane's Light Brigade marched, along with fifty troopers of the 20th Light Dragoons that led the brigade supported by three companies of riflemen. The first day's march south took some twenty-two hours, in heat that many of those confined aboard ship for so long found testing. Rifleman Harris wrote:

> We marched till it was nearly dark, and then halted for the night. I myself was immediately posted sentinel between two hedges, and in a short time General Fane came up, and himself cautioned me to be alert. 'Remember, sentinel,' he said, 'that we are now near an active enemy; therefore be careful here, and mind what you are about.'
>
> Next day the peasantry sent into our camp a great quantity of the good things of their country, so that our men regaled themselves upon oranges, grapes, melons, and figs, and we had an abundance of delicacies which many of us had never before tasted. Amongst other presents, a live calf was presented to the Rifles, so that altogether we feasted in our first entrance into Portugal like a company of aldermen.

Meanwhile, Wellesley issued orders for the other brigades to march on 10 August:

> G. O.   Lavos, 9th Aug. 1808.
> The army will march tomorrow by the right [senior brigade/battalion leading]; the mounted dragoons to lead, followed by the 3rd, 5th, and 4th brigades of infantry. The staff corps [are to] precede the column of infantry, and the dismounted dragoons to go to Lavos as a guard to the Commissariat. In addition to the dismounted dragoons, a captain's guard of fifty men, from the 4th Brigade, will remain as an escort to the military chest and the Commissariat stores.
>
> All other guards, piquets, and other duties, to be called in at an early hour in the morning; and the tents to be struck and packed in the cases, and the number of tents in each case to be marked upon them, in sufficient time to enable the whole line to move off at 4 o'clock. A small

BRITISH RIFLEMEN.

Hamilton Smith's picture of riflemen of the 5th 60th and 96th Rifles made up Fane's brigade.

guard to be left by each regiment in charge of the tents, for the purpose of loading them on the carts, and delivering them over to the Commissariat, after which the guards will proceed and join their regiments. Henceforth, with transport lacking, tents were not routinely available to the army when actively campaigning until 1813.

The artillery, dragoons, 45th and 91st regiments will receive 4 days' bread; the staff corps, the 3rd and 4th brigades, 3 days' bread, to complete them all to the 13th instant inclusive; and the whole will receive one day's meat, to be cooked this afternoon for to-morrow. The issue of these provisions to be made by the Commissary at 3 o'clock this afternoon . . .

Such corps as may have had any of their ammunition damaged will send requisitions, without delay, to the commanding officer of artillery for the number of rounds wanting to complete.

Three days' grain, and one day's straw for tomorrow, to be issued to-day by the Commissary to the artillery, cavalry, and other horses entitled.

Officers may receive money on account of their bat and forage allowance about to be issued, on application to the Deputy-Commissary-General.

ARTHUR WELLESLEY

The general order for the march was followed by further details as Wellesley issued the first of a whole series of memoranda giving detailed instructions as to how he wanted to conduct the campaign:

The formation of the column of march to-morrow morning: The dragoons to march off from their ground, and form half a mile in front of the artillery park by 4 o'clock A.M.

The 29th and 82nd to follow, and form with the head of their column upon the hill near the artillery park.

The staff corps, and the artillery of the 3rd Brigade, will form in the rear of the cavalry.

The 5th and 4th brigades will form with the head of their column upon the crossroad leading from their ground just on the right of the artillery, and will take their place in the column of march as it passes them.

The artillery will take care to be in front of the brigades to which they are attached.

The reserve artillery and depôt mules, &c., will follow the infantry; then the baggage of headquarters and General officers, the baggage of brigades in succession, the medical stores, the Commissariat mules, &c., depôts.

A captain to be left with the equipage, until carts take it off the ground, with a subaltern's guard from Brigadier-General Nightingall's brigade, a subaltern's guard from Brigadier General Bowes' brigade, and a serjeant and twelve privates from the 50th regiment. Men for this duty to be selected who are the least capable of marching.

If the camp equipage is got off the ground tomorrow, these guards will proceed forward and join their respective corps; if not, they will remain with the camp equipage until it is removed, and afterwards repair to Figueira, and apply to Captain Malcolm RN, for a transport to embark in.

ARTHUR WELLESLEY

Lieutenant General Sir Arthur Wellesley.

After two days' progress south, Wellesley again penned a General Order. This time he focused on the deployment of piquets and the conduct of the march:

G. O.   Leiria, 11th Aug. 1808.
The duties of field officer and adjutant to the piquets of the line are discontinued, and will be performed by brigades, commencing today. Each brigade to furnish both an outlying and inlying piquet of a captain and fifty men, with a proportion of officers and non-commissioned officers from each regiment, under the orders of a field officer of the brigade. Care to be taken that the sentries of the outlying piquets of each brigade are double, and communicate with those of the brigades or corps to their right and left whenever circumstances will admit of it. The General officer of the day will visit such of the piquets as he may think necessary, and they will receive their orders from him. All the field officers of piquets will report to him whenever anything particular occurs.

In column of march the light infantry companies of brigades will move at the head of their respective brigades, and be thrown out to either flank as circumstances may require.

The pioneers of brigades will also march in future at the head of their brigades in front of the light infantry companies, and the mules or horses conveying the camp kettles of companies, and the surgeons' field chest, and the bill hooks, will march in the intervals between the divisions, and be made to keep up with their respective corps. [This was found to be impractical causing the column to break up and the order was counter-manded several days later, with the mules, etc. thereafter being grouped at the rear of the brigade.]

The line of parade or defence of the brigades and corps will always be established when they take up their ground after a march; and if the troops are required to halt, they will make their huts as near to that line as possible.

Commanding officers of corps are referred to His Majesty's regulations respecting the number of batmen allowed to officers and will take care that is on no account exceeded.

A pint of wine per man to be issued this evening, at five o'clock, by the respective Assistant-Commissaries of brigades; and such corps as did not receive meat yesterday for to-day, will be supplied with it immediately. Meat for to-morrow to be issued to the army as soon after daylight in the morning as possible.

ARTHUR WELLESLEY

Two-Deep Line

Contrary to much opinion, the efficacy of deploying infantry battalions in two-deep line had been under discussion for some time before the Peninsular War. The two-deep line had been habitually used by the British in North America, but General Dundas, starting with *Principles of Military Movements* published in 1788 decreed a return to the Frederician three-deep line. However, in the war against the French two-deep line was again used during Abercrombie's Egyptian campaign in 1801. However, the C-in-C, the Duke of York, had issued a general order reminding the army that the three-rank deployment was still official policy. This was shortly relaxed somewhat when permission was given for inspecting officers to allow battalions to parade in two ranks, but with limited opportunities for the army to come to a consensus based on actual experience in battle, three-deep line remained official policy.

By 1808 Lieutenant General Sir Arthur Wellesley had some considerable military experience. As a junior officer he had served in the Low Countries during the War of the First Coalition, extensively campaigned in India, and had most recently commanded a brigade in Denmark. In all these campaigns the soldiers he led fought in the three-deep line as prescribed in Dundas's drill manual.[16]

The Battle of Maida is, despite earlier precedent and much discussion, held as the example of two-deep line. In 1806 the French invaded the Kingdom of Naples; as a result the people of Calabria rose in revolt. The British, seeking to foster further revolt, mounted a series of expeditions to the toe of southern Italy. When General Stuart landed, the French under General Reynier marched to confront him. The British army numbered around 5,500 men and the French with a slight numerical superiority 6,000. Stuart, although honoured for his victory at Maida, had an otherwise unremarkable command in the Mediterranean. His brigade commanders, however – Cole, Kempt, Oswald and Ross – as noted by Fortescue, were 'all men who made their mark later in the Peninsula'.

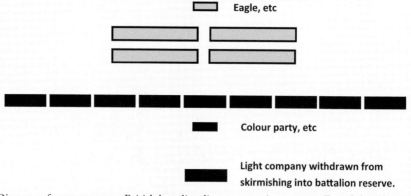

Diagram of a ten-company British battalion line *versus* a six-company French battalion in close column, with its grenadier and *tirailleur* companies detached as was the case in Junot's command in August 1808.

Two years later, John Crocker recalls that during a political meeting on the Dublin Water Pipe Bill in London on 14 June 1808, that Wellesley's mind was clearly on military matters, having that day been ordered to the Peninsula. Crocker noted that he had

> remained silent so long that I asked him what he was thinking of. He replied, 'Why, to say the truth, I am thinking of the French that I am going to fight. I have not seen them since the campaign in Flanders, when they were capital soldiers, and a dozen years of victory under Buonaparte must have made them better still. They have besides, it seems, a new system of strategy, which has outmanoeuvred and overwhelmed all the armies of Europe. 'Tis enough to make one thoughtful; but no matter: my die is cast, they may overwhelm me, but I don't think they will out-manoeuvre me. First, because I am not afraid of them as everybody else seems to be, and secondly, because if what I hear of their system of manoeuvres be true, I think it a false one as against steady troops. I suspect all the continental armies were more than half beaten before the battle was begun. I, at least, will not be frightened beforehand.'[17]

However much Wellesley was influenced by the Battle of Maida two years earlier, his own experience and the steadiness of British troops, he was clearly thinking about how he was going to fight the French with an open mind. On 3 August at Lavos in a General Order, Wellesley wrote: 'The order of battle of the army is two deep ...' The two-deep line was not a stand-alone solution to defeating the French, but combined with a deployment that offered secure flanks, protection from enemy artillery and skirmishers, it was certainly a part of the recipe for success of the British infantry during the Peninsular War.

British infantry deployed in two-deep line firing by sections. This produced a rolling fire down the line.

An officer of a line infantry battalion's light or flank company. He wears an 1806 pattern regimental cap with a green feather plume and flank company wings.

Chapter Three

The Affair at Óbidos

During 9 and 10 August 1808 Wellesley's army began its march south to Lisbon from the village of Lavos. For soldiers confined to ships for weeks, with only a few days to acclimatize, despite instructions that light marching order was to be adopted, for many in the summer heat it was a sore trial. Even though Dundas specifies the length of pace and the cadence of march, it is apparent that in the army's first few days en route south, a failure to maintain an even pace led to brigades on the march 'concertinaing'. This led those companies at the rear being alternately halted and the next minute running to keep up and struggling to maintain prescribed distances between units. Wellesley issued a GO at Calvario on 13 August to address this problem:

> It is the Lieutenant-General's desire that, in route marching a regular, steady pace should be preserved by the leading divisions of corps, without reference to those immediately preceding them. It is even desirable that each company or division should be led at a uniformly regular pace by its officer, without attention to the exact preservation of intervals, which is of less importance.

This instruction and others clearly worked, as on 16 August Wellesley wrote that the 'army is marching tolerably well'. Among the advance guard and marching with clear enthusiasm was Rifleman Harris:

> The next day we again advanced and being in a state of the utmost anxiety to come up with the French, neither the heat of the burning sun, or long miles … were able to diminish our ardour. Indeed, I often look back with wonder at the light-hearted style, the jollity, and reckless indifference with which men who were destined in so short a time to fall, hurried onwards to the field of strife; seemingly without a thought of anything but the sheer love of meeting the foe and the excitement of the battle.

Captain John Patterson of the 50th Foot in Caitlin Craufurd's brigade described the process of bivouacking on the march south:

> At the termination of each day's march, the troops were halted in the neighbourhood of wood and water. The alignment being taken up, and

the arms piled in column, fires were immediately put in requisition for cooking, and in a moment the clash and clang of bill-hooks and pioneers' entrenching tools resounded on every side; while the deep woods rang again with the clamour of ten thousand tongues, and the harsh discordant sound of bugles, drums, and other noisy accompaniments, producing, on the whole, a scene not unworthy of Hogarth himself, who might have been aroused from the dead to execute the task of depicting it had he been entombed within the precincts of our turbulent camp.

Before daylight the army was up, and standing to their arms, formed in open column, the reveille at the same time was sounded from right to left, and echoed through the closely planted hills, giving to our enemies in the front loud intimation of our near approach, and proving that his newly arrived visitors were at all events on the alert, and came early into the field.

The first few days of Brigadier General Fane's march were through scrubby pine woods, in arid sandy country, 'occasionally varied by uncultivated heaths, with here and there a vineyard'. It took three days for the army's advance guard to reach the area of Leiria. During these marches the first shot fired in the six years of war in the Peninsula was a friendly-fire incident during the hours of darkness. A corporal of the 20th Light Dragoons on a forward patrol was investigating a potential ambush position and was shot in the arm on his return by a trooper who mistook him for an enemy vedette. This prompted the rest of Fane's brigade in some haste to deploy astride their road in expectation of attack, which wasted time before it was discovered that it was a false alarm.[1]

At Leiria, arriving ahead of the British, the Portuguese seized a French magazine. Napier complains that they did this 'without making any distribution to the British' but as an *ad hoc* force their need was certainly greater than that of Wellesley's army. Having arrived in the town, the British rounded up deserters from a Swiss regiment garrisoning Peniche. Captain Leach recalled:

> Leaving Leiria, we marched in the direction of Lisbon, our advanced guard being in constant expectation of coming up with detached parts of the enemy, who were known to be falling back gradually as we advanced. As yet, the only specimens of the French army which we had seen were five Swiss deserters, from their infantry, clothed in scarlet, and remarkably fine-looking men. The time, however, was at hand, when we were to see and to have a brush with them.

The Swiss told Fane, who was under orders not to get involved in action with the enemy, that the French had abandoned Leiria. Consequently, he marched

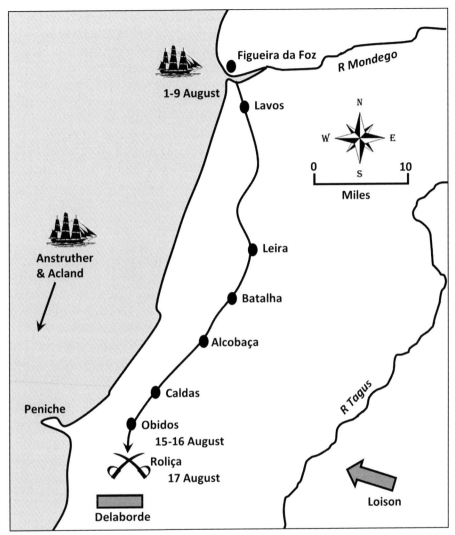

General Wellesley's landing and advance from Mondego Bay to Roliça, 9–16 August 1808.

on the town where the sights that greeted the brigade were appalling. Captain Leach saw and recorded evidence of French brutality in Leiria:

> which had, a short time before, been visited by a considerable French force, detached from Lisbon to levy contributions on the different towns. Here they were guilty of atrocities which exceeded belief. The town bore every mark of recent depredation, plunder, and excess of all kinds. The walls of a convent, into which I went with some other officers, were covered with blood and brains in many places; damning proofs of

the scenes which had been recently acted there, in spite of the attempts made by some persons to exculpate the French, and to prove the assertions of the Portuguese exaggerated. What unprejudiced person, who has served in the Peninsular war, will say, that an exaggeration of facts is necessary to rouse feelings of indignation against the French for their countless acts of merciless cruelty towards the people of Spain and Portugal?

At Leiria there were disagreements between *Marechal de Campo* Freire and General Wellesley over the capture of the Leiria magazine, the campaign

The red-coated soldiers of 1st Battalion 4th Swiss Regiment in French service.

plan, routes and the supply of rations to the Portuguese by the British. Wellesley reported to Castlereagh:

Before I marched to Leyria [*sic*], the Portuguese officers earnestly urged my early advance, to secure a magazine which had been formed at that place, as I understood, for the use of the British troops, and my advance certainly saved it from the enemy. But I received no supply from the magazine, which was left entire for the use of the Portuguese army. On the evening, however, of the arrival of the Portuguese army at Leyria, some very extraordinary messages were sent to me respecting their supplies; and in a conversation which I had with him that night, General Freire expressed his anxiety upon the subject.

The plan of the march for the next morning was communicated to him, and the hour for the departure of the Portuguese troops was fixed. Instead of making the march, however, as had been agreed upon, I received from General Freire a proposition for a new plan of operations, which was to take the Portuguese troops to a distance from the British army, by Thomar, towards Santarém, unless I should consent to feed the whole of them; and the pretext for the adoption of this plan was the probable want of supplies on the road which I had proposed to take, and their great plenty in the proposed quarter; and that the Portuguese troops would be in a situation to cut off the retreat of the French from Lisbon.

In my reply, I pointed out the inefficiency and danger of this plan, and requested the General to send me 1,000 infantry, all his cavalry, and his light troops, which I engaged to feed; and I recommended to him either to join me himself with the remainder, or at all events to remain at Leyria, or at Alcobaça, or somewhere in my rear, where at least his own troops would be in safety. He has sent me the troops which I have required, to the amount of 1,400 infantry, and 260 cavalry; but he has announced to me that he intends to persevere in his proposed plan of operations for the remainder of his army; notwithstanding that I have informed him that I have found resources in the country fully adequate to the subsistence of his troops.[2]

Having found the resources of the country more ample than I expected, I should certainly have undertaken to feed his army according to his desire; as I consider it of importance, on political, rather than on military grounds, that the Portuguese troops should accompany our march; only that I have found the British Commissariat to be so ill composed as to be incapable of distributing even to the British troops the ample supplies which have been procured for them; and I did not wish to burden them with the additional charge of providing and distributing supplies to the Portuguese army. Besides, as I have above explained to your Lordship, I do not believe the motive stated is that which has caused the determination to which I have adverted.

Despite Wellesley's attempts to persuade Freire to remain alongside him as a concentrated force, the Portuguese commander decided that he would advance on a separate axis further inland. Dom Miguel Pereira Forjaz, a member of Freire's staff, supports views that there was more to the refusal to advance beyond Leiria than the Portuguese general claimed:

> Nor was it from fear of meeting the French or jealousy of command, as some historians have speculated. The refusal was based upon the opinion that the main objective of the Portuguese army could not be solely to occupy Lisbon while the strong possibility existed that there would be a need to protect the provinces from the ravages of the French army, should it withdraw from the capital.[3]

Having been forced to leave behind tents and such heavy baggage that they had for want of adequate transport in favour of food and ammunition, the British continued their march south from Leiria on 14 August.

While General Wellesley's army was marching south, Delaborde with his delaying force had set out from Alcobaça and reached Batalha. It had been his intention to make his first stand here, but there was no suitably strong defensive position from which he could take on the numerically superior British force. Without the surety of being able to withdraw safely, Delaborde retraced his steps back to Roliça, leaving company-strength outposts around the hilltop village of Óbidos.

It was during the afternoon of 14 August that Fane's advance guard approached Alcobaça and passing an abandoned bivouac site, they found that they had missed the French by less than an hour, as evidenced by the food including meat that the enemy had abandoned in their haste to get away. Fane's brigade was, however, ordered forward another mile and to deploy piquets to cover the rest of the army, which to the annoyance of the brigade was comfortably ensconced in the town enjoying Portuguese hospitality.

The Affair at Óbidos

The following day the army marched for Caldas, while Fane's advance guard under Major Travers pushed on the extra few miles towards Óbidos, which Wellesley wanted in his hands. In the late afternoon, fifty troopers of 20th Light Dragoons and three companies of riflemen, two of the 5th 60th and No. 3 Company of the 2nd 95th approached the small walled town of Óbidos, which stands on a steep rocky ridge above a plain. It was here that Sergeant Landscheit of the 20th Light Dragoons first encountered a French battalion deployed in piquets across the front and commented that 'They were in possession of the town when we arrived in front of it, and presented

Employment of Light Companies

Light infantry was a branch of Britain's Georgian army that had undergone a renaissance since the revolutionary wars. Dundas's manual had just a single page referring to light infantry drill and manoeuvres, but De Rottenburg's manual had been translated at the turn of the century and Captain Cooper had in 1806 published a collection of works on light infantry tactics. The Peninsular War would, however, see a further development in such tactics.

Among the numerous General Orders issued by General Wellesley, one of the first was circulated at Lavos on 4 August:[4]

> The Lieutenant-General requests the General officers commanding brigades will, on all occasions of march and formation of the line of their respective brigades, place the light infantry companies belonging to the several regiments under their command in a separate corps under the command of a field-officer. In the ordinary formation on parade, and in route marches, these corps of light infantry will be on the left of the brigade. In formation in front of the enemy they will be in front [normally deployed for skirmishing], or in rear, according to circumstances; and in the marches of columns to take up a position, they will be on the reverse flank of the column. The light infantry companies will, however, encamp, and do all duties with the regiments.

Such was the demonstrable utility of light infantry and their close cousins the Rifles, on campaign and in battle, that further light battalions were raised during the course of the Peninsular War. Colonel Campbell of the 95th Rifles and the 54th Foot wrote a full new manual of 1,111 pages plus diagrams in 1807 with a second edition in 1813.[5] The same year in the Royal Military Panorama the following was published based on peninsular experience:

Light Company detached: The light companies are detached under the command of an experienced Field-Officer, who must be well acquainted with light-infantry movements, to form the advanced-guard, to cover the column during its march, and to mask the several evolutions of the brigade.

The brass bugle horn badge as worn on the 1806 pattern regimental cap by light battalions, rifles and soldiers of line battalions' light companies.

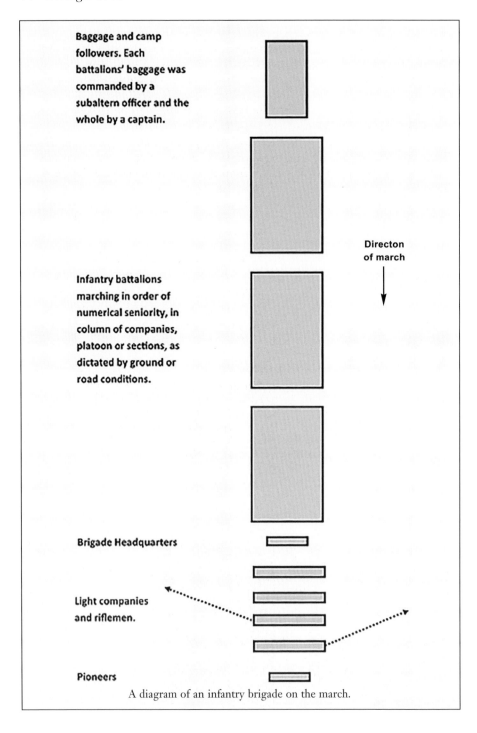

Baggage and camp followers. Each battalions' baggage was commanded by a subaltern officer and the whole by a captain.

Direcon of march

Infantry battalions marching in order of numerical seniority, in column of companies, platoon or sections, as dictated by ground or road conditions.

Brigade Headquarters

Light companies and riflemen.

Pioneers

A diagram of an infantry brigade on the march.

Attention of the officer commanding the light companies: The chief attention of the officer commanding these companies must be directed to the several cautions which the General may give, previous to the intended movements of the brigade, and his own judgement must guide him in giving the necessary orders to the officers and men under his immediate command for their timely advancing or retreating, extending or closing, inclining to the right or left, &c. &c. so that the operations of the brigade may never be impeded by them.

Disposition of the light companies during the route march of the column: During the march of the brigade to the ground of exercise, one company will form the advanced-guard in the usual manner; another will move in open file along and at some distance from the pivot-flank of the column; and the third company in the same manner and distance on the reverse flank, detaching a Serjeant and a few men to form the rear-guard, so that the whole column is covered.[5]

a countenance so formidable, as to excite us in expectation of a stout resistance ...' The riflemen, however, quickly drove the French piquets from a windmill. There were, however, several windmills in the area and, given that the advance guard would be deployed on a wide front and that the French piquets would be similarly positioned, the story of windmills could be conflated or refer to that at the southern end of the Óbidos ridge, the Monte do

The small hilltop town of Óbidos overlooks the surrounding area.

Facho. Either way, at this point the enemy withdrew. Lieutenant William Cox of the 95th Rifles recorded that:

> On approaching the place, the enemy opened a fire of musketry from a windmill on a rising ground adjoining the place, and a few shots came from the town; however, a rapid advance of the Riflemen drew the French from all points of their posts, but being rather too elevated with this, our first collision with the foe, we dashed along the plain after them like young soldiers, but we were soon brought up by a body of French cavalry advancing from the main force.

Captain Landmann, an engineer on Fane's staff, on hearing firing was sent forward to establish what had been going on:

> … we learnt that the enemy had fired from behind an aqueduct at Óbidos, on our advance guard quite unexpectedly … which till then had concealed them. To the astonishment of the party they neither killed nor maimed a single man, nor even any of the horses. From this point they retired slowly, firing on our men.

Rifleman Harris was in Captain Leach's company as a part of the supports following the advance guard. He recalled that:

> It was on the 15th August when we first came up with the French. Their skirmishers immediately commenced operations by raining a shower of balls upon us as we advanced, which we returned without delay. The first

The aqueduct at Óbidos.

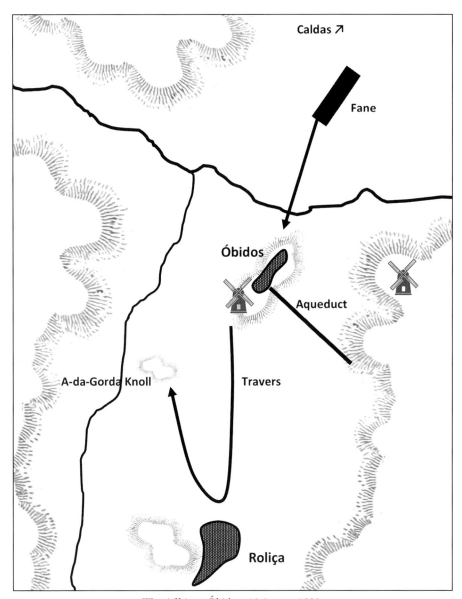

The Affair at Óbidos, 14 August 1808.

man hit was Lieutenant Bunbury. He was pierced through the head with a musket-ball and died almost immediately.

I had never heard such a tremendous noise as the firing made on this occasion, and I occasionally observed that the men on both sides of me were falling fast.

Having been shot at the beginning of the action, Lieutenant Bunbury became the first British soldier in the Peninsular War to be killed as a result of enemy action.

Having secured the environs of Óbidos, Major Travers pursued the enemy for between 2 and 3 miles, closing towards their main body. However, General Delaborde, standing on high ground west of Roliça, had seen the riflemen advancing beyond the support of the rest of their brigade into a vulnerable situation. He ordered his retiring piquets to stand their ground and dispatched an infantry battalion and some cavalry to envelop and cut off the riflemen. From the resulting counter-attack on both flanks, Travers extricated the advance guard with a swift withdrawal, only finally breaking clean with the help of the supporting companies that had been rushed forward. However, during a difficult withdrawal a number of riflemen were left behind and taken prisoner by the French.

Meanwhile, back at Caldas the sound of the action at Óbidos had the army standing to arms. Ensign Leslie of the 29th Foot later wrote:

> Soon after six o'clock in the evening of the 15th, the alarm was given that our outposts were engaged. Our brigade instantly turned out and marched off to support them. When we had got about 2 miles, we met General Sir Brent Spencer returning. He explained to us that a party of our 95th Rifle Corps had pushed on too far, and had got into contact with the French outposts, but that they had succeeded in driving the enemy from the long aqueduct and the old Moorish castle of Óbidos, of which they retained possession.

General Spencer marched Nightingall's brigade forward to cover the withdrawal of the rifles. However, they did not come into action as the threat of their presence alone halted the French pursuit. The rifles were pulled back and deployed Leach's company as a piquet on the A-da-Gorda Knoll at a more traditional distance forward of the main body. Rifleman Harris wrote:

> We retired to a rising ground, or hillock, in our rear, and formed there all round its summit, standing three deep, the front-rank kneeling. In this position we remained all night, expecting every moment that the whole host would be upon us.
>
> At daybreak we received instructions to fall back as quickly as possible upon the main body. Having done so, we lay down for a few hours' rest, before again advancing to feel for the enemy.

The losses in the action forward of Óbidos were in the 95th: in addition to Bunbury and three riflemen killed, Captain Pakenham and a rifleman were wounded and one was missing. The 5th 60th Rifles lost one man killed, five

The A-da-Gorda Knoll just over a mile south-west of Óbidos where the riflemen spent the night of 15/16 August.

On 16 August General Wellesley's headquarters was in the square at Óbidos.

A detachment of British infantry on the march from camp. Tentage was left behind thanks to a lack of transport and was not generally available to all ranks until the 1813 Campaign.

wounded and seventeen missing.[7] Wellesley's letter to the Duke of Richmond summed up the action:

> We had yesterday evening a little affair of advanced posts, foolishly brought on by the over-eagerness of the riflemen in the pursuit of an enemy's piquet, in which we lost Lieutenant Bunbury of the 95th killed and Pakenham slightly wounded, and some men of the 95th and 60th. The troops behaved remarkably well, but not with great prudence.[8]

Chapter Four

The Combat of Roliça

Following the affair around Óbidos, the 16th was spent with the army closing up to the town of Caldas and reconnaissance. Captain Landmann of the Royal Engineers, attached to the staff of Fane's brigade, was one of those officers who rode forward to view the ground up to Roliça and establish the road layout as the army had few maps and those available were invariably inaccurate:

> My first object was to reconnoitre the whole of the surrounding country. Having very quickly inspected the ground on the West, I crossed the valley to the Eastward of the town by following the side of the aqueduct, where there is a good road leading over the hills by some windmills, and in a direction which I suspected might again join, or in some way communicate, with the more direct road to Lisbon, which is by Roliça. Having questioned several of the country people to that effect, they confirmed me in my conjecture, assuring me that this road rejoined the high road to Lisbon, at some distance beyond the tops of the hills of Columbeira, on which the enemy was then posted.
>
> The hills of Columbeira presented a strong front of steep and broken ground, covered with pine trees towards Óbidos, and at the distance of about 6 miles from that place.[1]

The following morning, having bivouacked alongside Fane's small battery of guns, Landmann was in conversation with the battery commander:

> The bugle sounded at about two o'clock on the morning of the 17th, when Geary ordered his breakfast to be got ready forthwith, and as we sat on the very wet grass, drinking our cup of tea, and eating a slice of bread and butter, by the light of a small lanthorn, he asked me many questions as to the result of my reconnaissance of the preceding day; and particularly, if I thought we should come to any engagement on that day; to the latter I replied that I was decidedly of opinion, the enemy intended to defend the position which they occupied on the hills of Columbeira, so we should in all probability be on that day engaged.

Captain Landmann, as an experienced soldier who had spent the previous day in detailed reconnaissance, was not wrong.

Captain George Landmann, Royal Engineers.

Shortly after dawn, General Wellesley was forward to join the outposts in Óbidos accompanied by some of his staff, as recalled by Captain Landmann:

I proceeded to the high Moorish tower at the southern angle of the town [of Óbidos], from the top of which I occupied myself in examining the position occupied by the enemy; and with the aid of my telescope, I could distinctly see them moving about on the brow of the hills of Columbeira, beyond the town of Roliça.

Whilst thus engaged, I suddenly heard the sound of footsteps of several persons behind me, and also the scraping of scabbards, which indicated the presence of staff officers. I immediately heard a voice asking hastily in a voice of authority for a glass, and at the same moment I was tapped on the shoulder and desired to make room, for the space was very small and insufficient for two persons to rest their glasses, so as to observe the enemy at the same time. I now, as required, turned round, and Sir Arthur Wellesley was before me; upon which I presented my telescope to his Excellency.

Sir Arthur took a very careful survey of the country, as far as it was possible from that spot, and particularly examined the position occupied by the enemy; after which I related to him my reconnaissance of the preceding day, principally in regard of the hills to the Eastward, adding that I fully believed from my own observation, and also from the information I had obtained, that the road I had there followed up to the two windmills, led to the rear of the enemy's position, round his right flank, and therefore offered a good opportunity for cutting off his retreat; whilst at the same time, a movement by that route would intercept the expected junction of General Loison with Laborde [*sic*]; the former being understood to be on his march from Thomar, or its vicinity, with 6,000 men, and the latter occupying the hills of Columbeira in our front.

Sir Arthur Wellesley appeared to be satisfied with my communication, and not displeased at the liberty I had used in making the above suggestion; for he immediately ordered Major-General Ferguson and Brigadier-General Bowes, with their brigades, and the artillery of the Light Brigade, to march by the road I had spoken of to him; and then said to me; 'As you have reconnoitred that country, you will go with Ferguson.'[2]

The French, numbering 2,500 men, were deployed astride a broad low hill immediately to the west of the village of Roliça, half a mile forward of a substantial horseshoe of hills, the rugged Heights of Azambujeira (also referred to as the Heights of Columbeira).

Ensign Leslie of the 29th was among those in the centre waiting to be put in motion:

Here the whole army was formed in mass, each brigade in [a line of] contiguous columns of battalions at half distance ... While we were in this position a careless observer would not, perhaps, have noticed anything particular. He would have seen the arms piled, and the men occupied as they usually are on all occasions of a morning halt – some sitting on their knapsacks, others stretched on the grass, many with a morsel of cold meat on a ration biscuit for a plate in one hand, with a clasp knife in the other, all doing justice to the contents of their haversacks, and not a few with their heads thrown back and canteens at their mouths, eagerly gulping down his Majesty's grog, or the wine of the country, while others, whiffing their pipes, were jestingly promising their comrades better billets and softer beds for the next night, or repeating the valorous war-cry of the Portuguese.

But to a person of reflecting mind there was more in this condensed formation than a casual halt required. A close observer would have noticed the silence and anxious looks of the several general officers of brigades, the repeated departure and arrival of staff-officers and *aides-de-camp*, and he would have known that the enemy was not far distant, and that an important event was about to take place.[3]

Awaiting Wellesley's advance, Delaborde's situation was unenviable, not least because with just 4,350 men he would be outnumbered at least three to one if he stood and fought. If he withdrew rather than fight at a numerical disadvantage, there were three equally unpalatable choices. He would either expose to a British advance the Torres Vedras Road, or the direct route to Lisbon, or he would lose communication with Loison and his expected reinforcement. True to his orders from General Junot, Delaborde elected to fight a delaying action at Roliça despite the disparity in numbers. Napier, however, commented that 'encouraged by the local advantage of his position, and justifiably confident in his own talents, Delaborde resolved to abide his enemy's assault …'[4]

On a low hill north of Roliça, Delaborde deployed a single battalion each of the 70th *Ligne*, 2nd and 4th *Légère*, a half-battalion of Swiss infantry and the five light guns of his artillery; sufficient a show to force Wellesley to deploy and consume time.

The 'advantage of his position' was that Delaborde could quickly withdraw his small light force from his initial ground at Roliça up to a formidable position from which a small, outnumbered force could mount a successful delaying action – one that could also be costly for the enemy to attack – and Delaborde was still expecting Loison's division to arrive from the south-east during the day. This division was, however, still to the north-east marching the 15 miles from Alcoentre.

At 0700 hours the British army began the 8-mile march from Caldas to Roliça. According to Ensign Leslie of the 29th, 'final arrangements having been made for the attack, the army was put in motion.' William Napier wrote: 'Early on the morning of the 17th, thirteen thousand four hundred and eighty infantry, four hundred and seventy cavalry, and eighteen guns, issued from Óbidos, and soon afterwards broke into three distinct columns of battle.'

General Wellesley's plan was to use his superior numbers in a double envelopment of the French, with a strong column on the left led by Ferguson and his brigade, supported by Bowes' brigade (the 2nd and 4th brigades), plus another three companies of the 5th 60th Rifles. One of the reasons for the strength of the left column – almost 5,000 men and a battery of guns – was to cover the possible intervention of Loison's force from the east, which Wellesley's intelligence had placed at Rio Mayor on the 15th. The right flank column consisted of the 1,000 infantry and 50 cavalry of Colonel Trant's Portuguese detachment that had been left with Wellington by General Freire. The orders for both Trant and Ferguson were to turn the flanks of the French who were deployed on some rising ground south-west of the village of Roliça.

In the centre Wellesley massed some 9,000 troops in four brigades of infantry, plus an Anglo-Portuguese force of 400 cavalry, to attack the French position on the low hill west of Roliça. Each taking a separate road south from Óbidos, Hill's brigade was to form three battalion columns on the right and Nightingall's brigade two columns on the left. Caitlin Craufurd's three battalions followed behind Nightingall in reserve. Fane's brigade, consisting of four companies of the 2nd 95th Rifles under Major Travers and seven of the 5th 60th, numbering 1,000 men, were to deploy for skirmishing to the left of centre. They would to an extent bridge the gap between Nightingall's brigade and Ferguson's command on the left flank. If all went well, Wellesley's frontal attack would fix Delaborde in position, while the flanking manoeuvres would cut off his withdrawal, leading to complete destruction or capitulation.

The Advance on Delaborde's First Position

General Foy wrote that 'At nine in the morning of the 17th, a musketry was heard towards the advanced posts on the right. The English army mobbing out of the passes.' The fire heard by the French on their right was the skirmishers of Fane's brigade advancing against the French outposts. Foy described the approach of the British across the rough ground of the plain:

> They marched slowly but with order continually closing up gaps which were made by the obstacles of the ground and converging towards the narrow position of the French. In this spectacle there was something striking to the imaginations of young soldiers who, till then, had never had to do with anything but bands of fugitive insurgents.[5]

The French centre or fusilier companies, where most of the inexperienced soldiers were concentrated, were about to face their first real battle. Their battalions had, however, been weakened by the practice of forming elite battalions, as Foy explained:

> The flanks of the battalions were not supported by the grenadiers and light troops, these having, for the greater part, been formed into a picked regiment. The strength of this corps [the fusilier companies] consisted wholly in the talents of its leaders, and especially in the coolness and energy of the General, an old warrior, beloved by the soldiers, and quick in inspiring them with his own vigour and confidence.[6]

Rifleman Harris of the 2nd 95th Rifles was with the four companies of his battalion that joined the march initially with Ferguson's column from the outpost positions around Óbidos:

> On the 17th, being still in front, we again came up with the French, and I remember observing the pleasing effect afforded by the sun's rays glancing upon their arms, as they formed in order of battle to receive us.

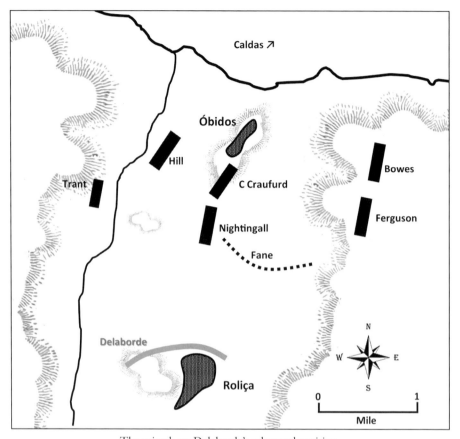

The miarch on Delaborde's advanced position.

Moving on in extended order, under whatever cover the nature of the ground afforded, together with some companies of the 60th, we began a sharp fire upon them; and thus commenced the Battle of Roliça.

William Ponton was a crony of mine. He was a gallant fellow and, having pushed himself in front of me, was checked by one of our officers for his rashness. 'Keep back you, Ponton!' the lieutenant said to him more than once. But in action Ponton was not to be restrained by anything but a bullet, and this time he got one. Striking him in the thigh, it must have hit an artery for he died quickly.

With Fane's brigade having deployed a skirmish line between the centre and Ferguson on the high ground to the left, as the columns in the centre approached the French position, Wellesley ordered his leading brigades to deploy their battalions into line. Hill's brigade inclined to the right and Nightingall similarly moved to the left, while Caitlin Craufurd's brigade

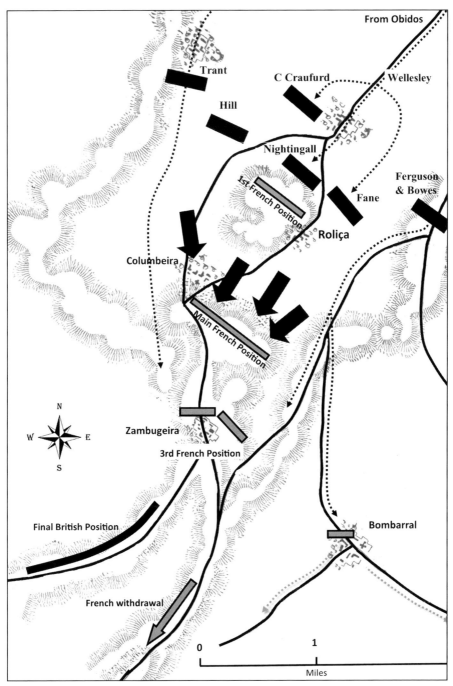

The Combat of Roliça.

halted as Wellesley's reserve. However, with the gap between Fane's riflemen and Nightingall's left flank being unconscionably great, the 45th Foot were immediately deployed from reserve to fill the ground. Rifleman Harris recorded details of the firefight with the French skirmishers:

> Soon afterwards the firing commenced, and we had advanced pretty close upon the enemy. Taking advantage of whatever cover I could find, I threw myself down behind a small bank, where I lay so secure, that, although the Frenchmen's bullets fell pretty thickly around, I was enabled to knock several over without being dislodged; in fact, I fired away every round I had in my pouch whilst lying on this spot.[7]

Wellesley's centre columns, with their bands playing, had deployed their artillery and opened fire, and the flanking moves of Ferguson and Trant became obvious. Consequently, having forced a deployment, Delaborde withdrew, to the disappointment of one Ensign Leslie who recalled:

> We made a momentary halt; the men were ordered to prime and load; we moved forward through the village of Mamed; after crossing a bridge, formed line and advanced, expecting to engage every moment. When we arrived at the position where we first saw the French posted, we found they had retreated. Their right was filing to the rear, masked by a cloud of skirmishers, posted on some rising ground covered with brushwood at the foot of the mountains, and warmly engaged with General Fane's riflemen.

Ferguson had been ordered to advance on a route via the ridge to the left that Captain Landmann had recced the previous day, which would turn the flank of Delaborde's position on the high ground. Landmann was, however, mortified when a staff officer galloped up ordering Ferguson's descent to the plain. The officer incorrectly told Ferguson that he was following a route that would fail to turn the French flank. Instead, the two brigades were to leave the ridge and advance on the French position near Roliça. This was one of the mistakes of the combat of Roliça that denied Wellesley a greater victory.

   With the British closing on Roliça, Foy described the French withdrawal from their forward position:

> As soon as the enemy was engaged in the plain, Delaborde judged that, if he obstinately defended Roliça, he should not leave time enough to fix himself in the strong position [on the Heights of Azambujeira] behind Columbeira. He sent the seventieth thither; and he himself retired to the entrance of the defile.

With him went the other two light infantry battalions along with the Swiss and the five light guns. Ensign Leslie continued: 'Their left had retired

Brigadier General Sir Henry Fane.

through the village of Columbeira, and occupied the heights of Roliça or Azambujeira, which ran in rear of and commanded that village.' The whole withdrawal was covered by the strong cavalry rearguard and the skirmishers of the 2nd and 4th *Légère* who fell back steadily in front of the riflemen. The four companies of the 2nd 95th were on the left and seven companies of the 60th Rifles were on the right of the long skirmish line. Having reached the heights, the French battalions deployed to the east of the road principally at the head of the four re-entrants, most of which were little more than gullies.

The Second French Position

The Heights of Azambujeira rise steeply between 350ft and 450ft above the plain with rocky crags that are still visible through today's more complete cover of fir trees. At the time of the battle, the ground cover was scrubbier in nature thanks to grazing. The four gullies, including that of Columbeira,

A view to the south from Roliça of the now tree-clad Heights of Azambujeira.

up which the modern route to Torres Vedras winds, gets narrower and the going rougher as one climbs, before gradually becoming less steep as the open country on the crest of the heights is reached. The Columbeira gully penetrated the left flank of Delaborde's second position, which was about three-quarters of a mile long.

With his first attempt at envelopment having failed, Wellesley regrouped his columns and set them marching as before in a repeat of his previous plan. Most maps of the battle show General Ferguson's command reclimbing the ridge to the left, but this is now debated. While remaining on the left flank he probably, at least initially, took a route across the lower slopes of the ridge, in touch with if not in supporting distance of Fane's brigade. Clearly while still on the lower slope Ferguson's battery fired the first ever shrapnel shells in anger. Captain Landmann was a witness:

> The battery being ready to open, [Colonel] Robe, near whom I was standing, turned to me, and asked what I considered the distance to be from our position to the enemy's line, in a rather oblique direction to our left, where the high road was seen winding into one of the ravines, and which appeared to be guarded by a Swiss regiment, with red coats and sky-blue facings. I answered that I thought the distance might be about 800 or 900 yards; upon which Robe observed, 'I think that must be very near the mark,' and added, 'I'll try a shrapnel at them for that range.' He accordingly ordered a fuze to be cut for 850 yards.
>
> I now took out my glass, and having ascertained the exact part of the line at which the gun had been pointed, I went a few yards to the left to clear the smoke, and when the shell was fired, it burst beautifully, at a

General of Division Henri-François Delaborde.

short distance, before it reached the line, upon which I immediately noticed a great number of the enemy drop on the ground. A second shell was discharged with similar result.

A pair of French 4-pounder enemy guns up on the high ground returned the fire with solid shot to no great effect.

On the British right flank, Colonel Trant and his Portuguese resumed their march south, on a line that would take his men up onto the high ground to the east of Columbeira. The brigade columns of Hill and Nightingall resumed their march towards the foot of the Azambujeira Heights, while Fane's riflemen 'hung on to' the French skirmishers 'and followed them up to the new position'.

As the centre columns followed the French, with Nightingall's brigade slightly more advanced than Hill's, they came under fire from *voltigeurs* posted among the rocks at the foot of the Azambujeira Heights' scarpe slope. Wellesley almost certainly would have wished to have the gullies that broke the slope cleared by the light companies of his leading brigades before attacks were launched and also to wait for the enveloping moves to bear fruit. However, the 29th Foot of Nightingall's brigade followed by the 9th of Hill's brigade, rather than demonstrating in Columbeira, pressed on up one of the gullies. Synchronization of disparate elements of an attack is always difficult, but it is accepted that Lieutenant Colonel Lake of the 29th advanced 'impetuously' with his battalion into the most significant gully well ahead of the other battalions of Hill's and Nightingall's brigades without waiting for them to come up in support. This gully branched into two separate dry watercourses about halfway up the slope.

Ensign Leslie described the advance of the right wing of his battalion: 'The 29th broke into open column, and advanced in column of sections through the village of Columbeira, led by the gallant Colonel Lake', and that 'On leaving the village the right wing turned to the left through some vineyards, and advanced along the foot of the heights in order to gain the pass, exposed to a flank fire the whole way, from which we suffered considerably.'

> They were now much galled by the enemy's sharpshooters from the heights, particularly from a high pinnacle commanding the village, and by a cannonade of round shot on the left. It being observed that the regiment was so much exposed, the left wing was ordered not to follow the right through the village, but to move round it to the left, and hence it did not reach the entrance of the pass until a considerable time after the right wing.

The light companies of the 5th, 29th and 82nd regiments had been detached 'to make a demonstration on a pass farther to the right', most probably that beyond Columbeira. Denied skirmishers to drive back their French *voltigeurs*, the 29th leading the brigade suffered particularly heavy casualties from the dominating Picoto feature during their march along the foot of the slope to their gully.

Watching the progress of the 29th Foot from Caitlin Craufurd's reserve position on the road north of Columbeira, Captain Patterson of the 50th recorded:

> Concealed within the close brushwood, on each side of the narrow defile, they took steady and deliberate aim, and their fire was attended with murderous effects. The 29th, however, commanded by the gallant Colonel Lake, pressed onward, to the gorge of the pass. While they were

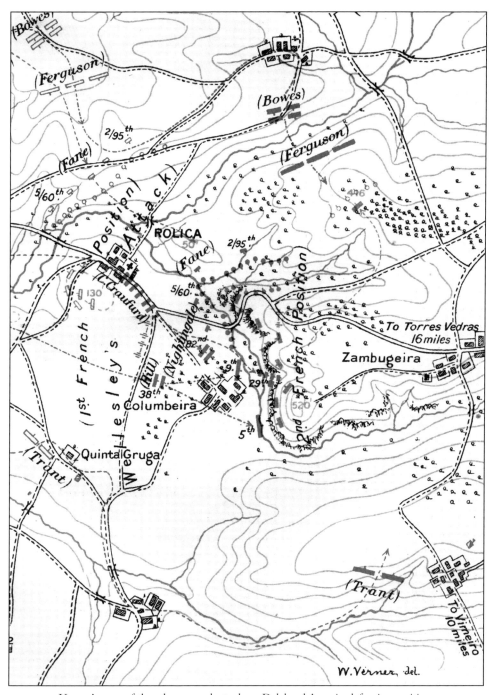

Verner's map of the advance and attack on Delaborde's main defensive position.

The gully just to the east of Columbeira that the 29th and 9th regiments attacked.

struggling up the rugged and precipitous ascent they were exposed to a shower of balls, and, in a few minutes, the grenadier company was nearly annihilated.[8]

The fire from French *voltigeurs* lining the gully was terrible. Leslie continued his account:

We now entered the pass, which was extremely steep, narrow and craggy, being the dried-up bed of a mountain torrent, so that at some places only two or three men could get up at a time. The enemy kept up a tremendous fire at point-blank upon us, to which not a shot was returned; but we kept eagerly pushing on as fast as circumstances would admit. About half-way up there was a small olive-grove, in which we halted to form, and the men were ordered to take off their haversacks, greatcoats, &c., which was done under a continual shower of bullets. The pass turned again very difficult; we could only advance by files, but no disorder took place, the men showing a laudable anxiety to push forward.

The farther we advanced the more the ravine receded into the centre of the enemy, and numbers were now falling from the continued fire on all sides.

Colonel Lake's horse was shot about this time, upon which Major Way dismounted, and gave up his horse to the colonel.

Napier states that the 29th took the left rather than the right branch of the gulley as intended, which would have seen them co-operating with Hill's brigade in capturing the 500ft Picoto, but the 9th Regiment of this brigade, thanks to the swift advance of the 29th, was still at the foot of the ridge.

Having passed through the second narrow defile, the leading companies of the 29th's right wing reached more open but still thinly wooded ground and the battalion again formed into line. 'The whole then pushed forward, and at last gained the wished-for heights; but we were now obliged, under a heavy fire, to take ground to the right.' This was to allow the left wing coming up behind the battalion room to join the battalion's line.[9] At this point it was not just the French skirmishers with which the 29th had to contend, but as Leslie recounts, a formed line as well:

When the enemy, who appeared to have been lying down behind a broken earthen fence, which ran rather in an oblique direction along our front, suddenly rose up and opened their fire, their officers seemed to endeavour to restrain them, and apparently urged them on to the charge, as we observed them knocking down the men's firelocks with their swords, but they did not advance.

At this stage the death of Lieutenant Colonel Lake brought a paralysis to the 29th's right wing, as Leslie explains:

Colonel Lake called out, 'Don't fire, men; don't fire; wait a little, we shall soon charge,' (meaning when more companies should come up), adding, 'the bayonet is the true weapon for a British soldier,' which were his dying words, for, as he moved towards the left to superintend the line being prolonged, he was marked and killed by a skirmisher … and his horse galloped into the French lines.

The right (in consequence of his death), not receiving any orders to advance, opened their fire, and a desperate engagement issued. Some of the enemy in front of the extreme right, either as a ruse or in earnest, called out that they were poor Swiss, and did not wish to fight against the English; some were actually shaking hands, and a parley ensued, during which the enemy's troops, who had been posted on the side of the ravine, finding we had forced it, and that they were likely to be cut off, began to retire, and coming in the rear of our right dashed through, carrying with them one major, who was dismounted, as before stated, five officers, and about twenty-five privates.

With most of the senior leadership captured or casualties and the 29th's right wing still under heavy fire from several directions and 'numbers decreasing very fast', the battalion's forward companies were paralysed. 'Major Egerton seeing the impossibility of making an effectual resistance, ordered us to fall back upon our left wing, which was still in the rear.' No doubt referring to this period, Foy wrote: 'There were even a few moments during which the

European Magazine

Engraved by Ridley & Blood from an Original Drawing by Andrews

The Hon.ble L.t Colonel George Augustus Frederic Lake

Published by J.Asperne at the Bible,Crown & Constitution,Cornhill,October 1.st 1808.

Lieutenant Colonel the Honourable George Lake prior to the campaign. He is wearing powdered hair and a queue, both of which were struck from regulations in July 1808.

29th laid down its arms in despair of escaping.' Despite their losses, the right wing retired into the cover of a scrubby wood through which they had earlier advanced:

On observing this the enemy set up a shout, and then, but not till then, advanced upon us, as if with a view to charge; some individuals on both sides got mixed, and had personal encounters with the bayonet; they, however, did not venture to press us, nor to follow us into the woody ground, where we formed on the left wing, which had now come up, being also joined by the 9th Regiment (which was sent to support the 29th when it was found that they were so seriously engaged). The whole now rapidly pushed forward and cleared the front of the enemy, who, after an ineffectual resistance, were driven from their position.

In his account of this period in the fighting General Foy states that 'Brigadier General Brenier charged at the head of the 1st Battalion 70th *Ligne*' and that he also 'dislodged the 5th Foot, which attacked on the side of Columbeira'.

Meanwhile, on the left of centre the riflemen of Fane's brigade were in action, having enveloped the determinedly held corner of high ground where the old road to Azambujeira and Torres Vedras climbed steeply from the plain. Captain Leach who commanded one of the 2nd 95th Rifles' companies noted that '... they again lay concealed, [keeping] up a running galling fire on us as we ascended.' Rifleman Harris of Captain Leach's company recalled: 'We had caught it pretty handsomely too for there was no cover for us, and we were rather too near. The living skirmishers were lying beside heaps of their dead, but we held our own till the battalion regiments came up.'

Rifleman Harris goes on to describe the death of his file partner while skirmishing during this phase of the combat:

> Joseph Cochan was by my side loading and firing very industriously about this period of the day. Thirsting with heat and action, he lifted his canteen to his mouth; 'Here's to you, old boy,' he said, as he took a pull at its contents. As he did so a bullet went through the canteen, and perforating his brain, killed him in a moment. Another man fell close to him almost immediately, struck by a ball in the thigh.

The riflemen were also under fire from the five French guns. Harris continued: 'I saw a man named Symmonds struck full in the face by a round shot, and he came to the ground a headless trunk. Meanwhile, many large balls bounded along the ground amongst us so deliberately that we could occasionally evade them without difficulty.'

At some point in the fighting the riflemen of the 60th 'gave way but Captain Bradford ADC to General Fane rallied them and brought them back into the line. In doing so, Bradford was mortally wounded.'[10] Matters were evened up when Captain Geary's battery of light 6-pounders reached the high ground, presumably by the old road. They were promptly in action, with a gun firing canister at a range of 60 yards contributing significantly to halting the French. With the immediate threat dealt with, two guns were again ordered to load shrapnel ammunition, which promptly put two of Delaborde's gun crews out of action in a successful engagement.[11] With the help of Geary's guns, the rifles gradually drove the *voltigeurs* back but, as Harris described: 'Having beaten them off the second hill and taken possession of it, the enemy retreated

French officers, 4th *Légère*.

to a wood – there being a valley between us and it – and recommenced a most tremendous fire, having received a reinforcement.'

This reinforcement was three companies from Delaborde's centre, which pushed the riflemen back off the crest of the ridge, but mounting persistent and effective rifle fire in turn forced the French to withdraw. Harris used the body of one of his comrades for cover:

> Of his dead body I made a rest for my rifle. Revenging his death by the assistance of his carcass, I tried my best to hit his enemies hard. There was no time to think either, for all was action with us Rifles at that moment. The barrel of my piece was so hot from continual firing that I could hardly bear to touch it, and I was obliged to grasp the stock beneath the iron as I continued to blaze away.

Meanwhile, back in Wellesley's centre, the British maintained pressure and renewed their assault, even though up on the high ground they were out-numbered by the French two to one, despite the arrival of the 45th Foot several hundred yards to the left. Having climbed the slope, this tired bat-talion soon found itself the target of several French guns. Ensign Dawson carrying the King's Colour was killed, along with men from the two centre companies that flanked the colour party. The 45th, however, did not advance to musket range of the French to return the fire.

Further west, however, General Brenier launched two further successful counter-attacks, but the determination of the 5th, 9th and 29th regiments of

The view across the country east of Roliça to the high ground along which Anstruther marched.

Riflemen deployed for skirmishing in scrubland. One man is primed and loaded while covered by his partner, who would only fire once his companion reported that he was 'loaded'.

foot told and the French were pushed back. Ensign Leslie records how the 29th had re-formed and took part in the advance to Azambujeira:

> I may state that after clearing the wood where we had re-formed, and were advancing in column of sections, a ball knocked off the steel of a sergeant's halberd, who was leading the section in front of me, which came flying backwards and struck Major Way, who, being dismounted, was walking alongside. Soon afterwards, when we were forming line, I saw his sword broken by a ball, whilst in the act of waving it and cheering the men. When he was taken prisoner, as before related, General Laborde [*sic*] gave him permission to retain the hilt of his sword, in which a part of the blade was still remaining; however, the escort (who behaved very brutally to him) afterwards made him throw it away.

The 82nd Foot was also engaged towards the end of the action. Lieutenant Wood of the 82nd was lucky not to be added to the casualty figures for his battalion:

> We now began to advance over those who had fallen: among them was my brother Sub[altern officer], who had been out skirmishing; and we came under what I then thought a pretty hot fire, both of fieldpieces and musketry, not having witnessed the like before: but this I found was a mere joke to what I was hereafter to experience. However, it gave me a seasoning – as I was soon after knocked down by a musket-ball striking

me on the left groin; and I only attribute escaping a severe wound to having some papers in the pocket of my pantaloons, which prevented its penetrating the flesh; but it caused a great contusion: I was, however, in a few minutes able to proceed with the regiment, and soon had the pleasure of seeing the French flying before us.[12]

The 20th Light Dragoons had hitherto been observers of the fighting, but with the British battalions established on the crest of the ridge they were deployed as described by Sergeant Landscheit:

We had watched the progress of the battle for some time, without sustaining any injury, except from a single shell, which, bursting over our column, sent a fragment through the backbone of a troop-horse, and killed him on the spot – when a cry arose, 'The cavalry to the front!' and we pushed up a sort of hollowed road towards the top of the ridge before us. Though driven from their first position [on the high ground], the enemy, it appeared, had rallied, and showing a line both of horse and foot, were preparing to renew the fight. Now, our cavalry were altogether incapable of coping with that of the French; and the fact became abundantly manifest, so soon as our leading files gained the brow of the hill – for the slope of a rising ground opposite was covered with them in such numbers, as to render any attempt to charge, on our parts, utterly ridiculous. Accordingly, we were directed to form up, file by file, as each emerged from the road – not in two ranks, as is usually done both on parade and in action – but in rank entire. Moreover, we were so placed, that the French officers could not possibly tell what was behind us; and thus made a show which appeared to startle them; for they soon

British infantry deployed in line.

began to change their dispositions, the infantry moving off first, the cavalry following: upon which we likewise broke again into column of threes and rode slowly after them.

At this stage General Ferguson's two brigades were to be seen on the left flank threatening to envelop Delaborde's force, but as Lieutenant Warre, ADC to General Ferguson noted: 'Our brigade having been sent to turn the [enemy's] right, arrived rather late, and were scarcely engaged. We lost a few men – five or six – and poor Capt. Geary of the artillery, after firing four shots at the enemy in most masterly style.'

This was the result of calling Ferguson down off the ridge to threaten Delaborde's first position when the centre brigades could have done the job of driving the French back. Doubt over the direction of the roads also played its part in this.

For the French, Delaborde's delaying action was over and it was time for another withdrawal, which was skilfully conducted at speed. The four French battalions leapfrogged back two at a time pursued by the British. They were covered by the 26th *Chasseurs à Cheval* who repeatedly advanced as if to charge, thus forcing riflemen and the light companies into rally orbs for protection or back on their supports. Nonetheless, Fane's riflemen followed the enemy towards the ridge-top hamlet of Azambujeira. Rifleman Harris described the culmination of the battle:

> There were two small buildings in our front. The French managed to get into them and therefore annoyed us much from that quarter. A small rise in the ground close before these houses also favoured them; and our men were handled very severely in consequence. So angry did they become that they would not stand it any longer. One skirmisher jumped up and rushed forward crying: 'Over boys! Over! Over!' Instantly the whole line responded with 'Over, over, over!' They ran along the grass like wildfire and dashed at the rise, fixing their sword-bayonets as they did so. The French light bobs, unable to stand the sight, turned about and fled. Having taken possession of their ground, we were soon inside the buildings.
>
> After the battle, the house I was in was soon well filled with the wounded – both French and English – who had managed to get there for a little shelter.

With Azambujeira cleared, the French marched away at a pace. James Todd of the 71st, a part of Ferguson's column, noted that:

> The engagement lasted until about four o'clock when the enemy gave way. We continued the pursuit until darkness put a stop to it. The 71st had only one man killed and one wounded. We were manoeuvring

An elite company trooper of the 26th *Chasseurs à Cheval* wearing a colback. The regiment had distinctive orange facings.

all day to turn their flank, so our fatigue was excessive, though our loss was small.[13]

Hitherto, Delaborde and Brenier, despite the former being wounded, had fought an admirable action, along with their officers, expertly timing their movements. Now, however, they were confronted with a narrowing of their route north as the road to Torres Vedras dipped into the river valley. With the British infantry marching in pursuit, the French fell into disorder as they

Maximilien Foy, the main French commentator on Roliça, as a younger man in the rank of *Chef de Bataillon*.

crowded together. Three of the five French guns were captured along with some prisoners, but without a decent-sized body of well-mounted cavalry, Wellesley was unable to mount an effective pursuit. The infantry complained that the cavalry were unwilling to charge, an accusation that Sergeant Landscheit's comments justify: 'But we [the outnumbered 20th Light Dragoons] had no desire to overtake them. They therefore pursued their march unmolested, except by a few discharges of cannon; and we, after seeing them fairly under way, halted on the field of battle.'

Delaborde continued his march north into the night as far as Montechique.

Aftermath

The reckoning, even for a small battle, was as grim as ever. The British lost 474 dead, wounded and taken prisoner; of these almost half belonged to the 29th Foot. The French lost around 600 men. Even though Wellesley's army

A representation of a trooper of a provisional dragoon regiment equipped for campaign.

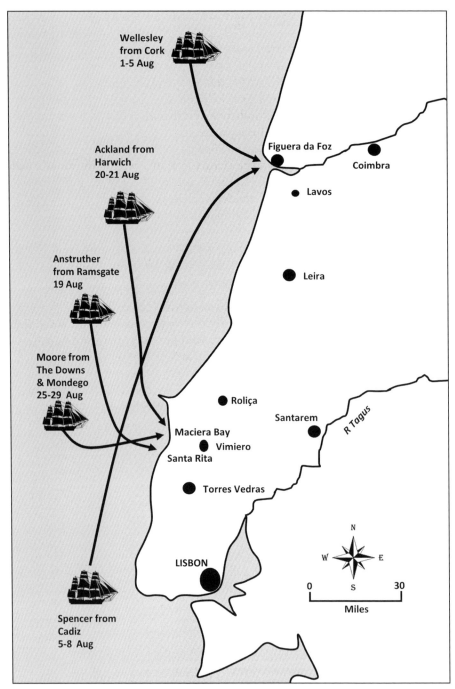

The places and dates of the arrival of elements of the British army in Portugal in 1808.

significantly outnumbered Delaborde's, the numbers that actually took part in the fighting were roughly equal to if not slightly in favour of the French.

Despite the failure of the enveloping moves and the precipitate attack on the gullies, Wellesley had successfully driven the experienced French from two defensive positions, but he had failed to destroy the smaller French force. On the other hand, Delaborde had suffered significant loss, but had demonstrated considerable skill and had inflicted a modicum of delay on Wellesley's progress south. Even though Wellesley's aim was the liberation of Lisbon and not the defeat of the French armies in Portugal *per se*, the delay was of little importance. The greatest effect of the victory at Roliça was on the morale and confidence of the allied soldiers. At the outset of the campaign, they had proved to themselves and to the French that they could beat the battalions of an army that had under Napoleon dominated Europe for more than a decade in what had been a difficult fight.

After the fighting, Ensign Leslie, one of three officers not killed, seriously wounded or captured from the 29th's right flank discovered how his commanding officer met his death:

> That Colonel Lake was killed by a sharpshooter was ascertained by the officers who were taken prisoners. There were two brothers named Bellegarde, forming part of the escort which conducted them to the rear. These brothers were eagerly disputing which of them had the honour of killing the colonel, one declaring that he was lying under a bush close to Colonel Lake, and deliberately shot him while he was giving orders and forming the line. The horse, as stated, sprang forward into the French line, where he was taken, and was afterwards returned to the regiment in the most handsome manner by General Laborde [*sic*], when we were doing duty in Lisbon with the French army, previous to their embarkation, in consequence of the Convention of Cintra.

Despite having marched all day and like many fought in his first action, Lieutenant Wood was one of the unlucky officers to be detailed for duty that night while surveying the aftermath of the fight:

> From reflecting on this mournful spectacle, I was soon diverted, by being ordered to go on the out-post of a field officer's piquet, about 2 miles in advance. I went out accordingly, and took my station behind a furze-hedge, from which I could hear French *videttes* talk plainly as I now hear the passagers under my window.

British Army Riflemen

By the turn of the century the experience of fighting swarms of French *tirailleurs* and *voltigeurs* in the Low Countries and taking on irregular troops in theatres of war such as the Caribbean once again brought the issue of British light infantry to the fore. Hitherto, reliance had been placed on largely German mercenary units to provide such troops. In 1797, during the reduction in the number of weak foreign corps, two such units – Lowenstein's and Hompesch's – were brought into the British line as the 5th Battalion, 60th North American Regiment. They were clad in the famous green jacket and armed with a rifle.[14]

Two years later Colonels Coote Manningham and Stewart were leading proponents of a British rifle-armed light infantryman and in January 1800 a third iteration of an Experimental Rifle Corps was formed. A competition between gunsmiths resulted in the adoption of the 1800 Pattern Short Infantry Rifle, otherwise known as the Baker Rifle. The stated aim was to provide trained cadres for fifteen line infantry battalions, but following the highly creditable performance of the newly trained riflemen during the Ferrol expedition and subsequent dispersion of the corps, a battalion of what would become the 95th Rifles was formally raised in January 1801.

Training of riflemen and their officers in light infantry tactics was based on a translation of De Rottenberg's manual. Unlike their musket-armed line counterparts who 'fired into the brown', riflemen spent as much time on marksmanship as

Baron de Rottenberg, whose manual for light infantry was used by the rifle regiments as the basis of their tactics.

A picture from *The Illustrated Manual of Rifle Drill and Firings 1804* printed by J.T. Smith.

on the drill square. They fired on the range with targets out to 300 yards, with marks of distinction being awarded to the best shots. A light infantryman, even one with a rifle, had to master the full Dundas drill as well as that of light infantry, but above all, to develop initiative. Deployed in a far looser chain, often away from officers and NCOs, the rifleman needed to develop and be trusted with initiative that was rare in all but the light companies of some line battalions.

A second battalion of the 95th was raised in 1805, and initially in 1808 half of the army's three battalions of riflemen – the 5th 60th and four companies of the 2nd 95th Rifles – deployed with Fane's brigade in Wellesley's army from Cork. They would shortly be joined later in the campaign in Portugal by two companies of the 1st 95th Rifles in Acland's brigade. A third battalion of the 95th was raised in 1809 and later in the war every company of rifles was deployed in the Peninsula less some depot companies.

In the aftermath of the combat of Roliça, General Wellesley made one of his most significant adjustments to his army's order of battle. While preserving Fane's 'Light Brigade', he made provision for each brigade to have a company of riflemen, a practice he maintained throughout the war:

> The following new distribution of brigades to take place on leaving this ground. The 6th or light brigade to consist of the 50th Regiment, four companies of the 95th and five companies of the 60th. One company of the 60th to be attached to each of the following brigades: the 1st, 2nd, 3rd, 4th, and 5th and to join them as soon as possible.[15]

This measure would enhance the skirmishing capacity of his brigades by the addition of the longer range of the 1800 Pattern Short Infantry Rifle.

One of the main duties of the rifle battalions was to provide the army's outposts and piquets. Unlike much of the rest of the army, they were well trained in this essential activity, but there were plenty of practicalities for them to learn through experience.

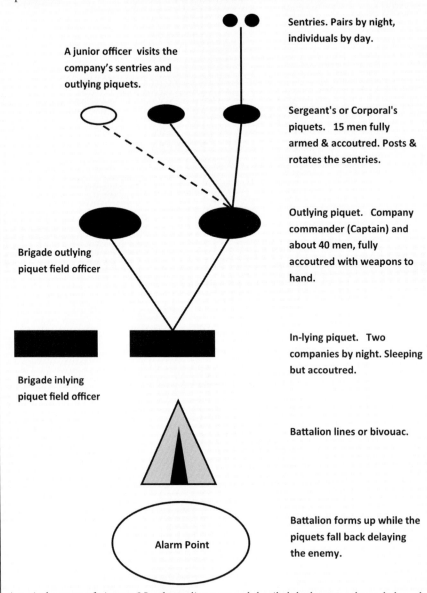

A typical system of piquets. Numbers, distances and detailed deployment depended on the ground, weather, availability of troops and the tactical situation.

Chapter Five

Piquets and Preparations for Battle

Wellesley was originally intending to continue his march south from Roliça and position himself between Delaborde and Loison. However, that aim was overtaken by events, as on the evening of 17 August word reached him that the expected reinforcements of Acland's brigade had arrived from England off Peniche, and had been directed to Maceira Bay. Anstruther's brigade was expected to follow shortly afterwards. In anticipation of the arrival of the reinforcement Wellesley stuck to the coast road in his march south, but this course still took him within a day's march of the assembling French army.

On 17 August Loison with his division of almost 6,000 men was joined at Cerecal by General Junot. He had finally marched from Lisbon on the 15th with just 2,000 men, having left what is considered to have been an unnecessarily large garrison of 6,500 men in the city. A median figure for estimates of the size of Junot's army immediately before Vimeiro is around 13,000 with approximately 10,000 infantry, 2,000 cavalry and 26 guns. The original French formations had been much depleted by detaching garrisons across the country and needed regrouping into reasonably balanced brigades and divisions, which took place during this period. (See Appendix VII for Orders of Battle at Vimeiro.)

While at Cerecal, the two French generals heard the thunder of cannon at Roliça, but being on the march more than 10 miles away, they were too far away to intervene. On 19 August Junot fell back south to Torres Vedras and was joined by Delaborde the following day. With the numerous French cavalry scouring the country for information, during the 20th reports reached Junot that of the two roads south, the British were concentrated on the coast road. Based on these reports, Junot made his decision to attack, and on the night of 20 August his troops started the 10-mile march to Vimeiro. He sent his divisions on their way with the words 'Soldiers, you only have to march and meet these cowardly islanders to drive them into the sea.'

Despite the outcome of Roliça and probably aware that he was outnumbered, General Junot, according to Captain Patterson of the 50th Foot, was confident of victory:

Junot, who was general in chief, held the British in much contempt, and endeavoured to impress upon the minds of his followers, that their

81

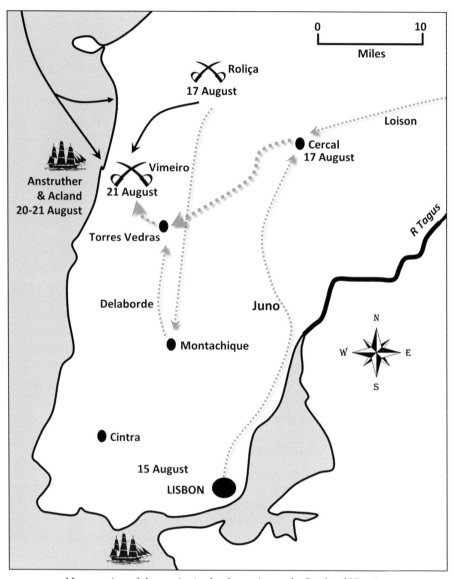

Manoeuvring of the armies in the days prior to the Battle of Vimeiro.

antagonists were a set of raw campaigners, wholly devoid of military skill. From the testimony of some deserters, who came into our lines, we learned, that the Marshal [*sic*] intended, before many days were over, to give us a dusting, and to brush the pipeclay out of our jackets. This cavalier determination of the Marshal afforded no small amusement to our soldiers, who promised themselves some good sport, whenever the gasconading Frenchman might be pleased to make true his words: and, not to be behindhand with him in kindness, they resolved gratefully to return the compliment, by trimming the whiskers of his gallant veterans, and powdering their mustachios, in so artist-like a manner, that the aid of a *friseur* should no longer be required.[1]

General Foy, however, notes that there were other factors that propelled Junot into action, namely the nascent revolt in Lisbon and the fact that the British would only get stronger with time.[2] General Junot's boasts had been passed on to British officers during those contacts between opposing piquets that abounded particularly in the early part of the war. The combat at Roliça had provided some confidence, but there were 'croakers' in Fane's Light Brigade, who dismissed Wellesley's successes in India and 'stated we shall most probably be all cut to pieces; and so Junot may say with truth he will make the pipeclay fly out of us.'[3]

Meanwhile, Wellesley had marched south via Lourinha towards Vimeiro. It was during this time that Lieutenant Wood of the 82nd Foot of Nightingall's brigade recalled that he:

... was now, for the first time, on an out-post before the enemy; no covering but my greatcoat – no pillow but my cocked hat. The fine ornaments which had shone so conspicuously on the parades on home service began to lose their brilliancy: the glittering epaulette was crushed into a thousand forms, and the pretty tight boot cut with many a slit to ease the blistered foot. Most glad was I to feel the morning sun warm my dewy limbs; and, hardly had it made its appearance, when we were called in, and had but just time to get a little warm tea, so refreshing to the weary frame, when off we marched in pursuit of the enemy, whom we followed up for a few days, till we reached the field of Vimeiro, where we halted some time.[4]

Wellesley's army reached Vimeiro on 19 August to await the landing of the reinforcing brigades and he reported that he had deployed:

In order to be more certain of protecting the disembarkation of General Anstruther's brigade, which I expected would have been made at Maceira. Brigadier General Anstruther landed on that evening, and in the night of the 19th and 20th, about 8 miles north of Maceira, and joined on the morning of the 20th.[5]

There could, however, have been a disaster on a dangerous lee coast. Captain Malcolm of HMS *Donegal* explained to the Cintra Inquiry:

On the 20th August the wind came from the south-west. I weighed and made the signal for the convoy so to do – the convoy then consisted of

HMS *Donegal* was a French-built ship captured in 1798 and taken into service with the Royal Navy.

230 or 240 vessels. About one half of the convoy succeeded in getting under weigh, the others were obliged to remain at anchor. Next day the wind shifted, and on my return to Maceira Roads I found about sixty of the convoy had lost their anchors in attempting to weigh, and I have no doubt had the breeze increased to a common gale that many of the vessels would have been lost; they were then mostly reduced to their last anchor, and the bottom is very rocky.[6]

The landing of Anstruther's brigade on the adjacent Santa Rita Bay was if anything rougher than at Marcia Roads with, for example, the 2nd battalions of the 43rd and 52nd Light Infantry getting a good soaking.[7]

Wellesley had not only to look to the deployment of the army, but at this stage its administration as well. In a General Order written on the 20th he made provision for transport and cooking for Anstruther's brigade which had sailed without full campaign equipment:

The several regiments of infantry will forthwith send into the Deputy Commissary-General twenty camp kettles each, for the purpose of supplying the 7th brigade, who are unprovided with them; and the 95th will, for the same object, furnish eight camp kettles. As soon as the whole are collected, the Deputy Commissary-General will issue an equal proportion of them to the 2nd battalions of the 9th, 43rd, and 52nd regiments, and the 97th regiment, and will allot to each of those corps one cart for the conveyance of the kettles.[8]

Deployment

The halt at Vimeiro was intended to be temporary before resuming the march on Torres Vedras. In a dispatch to the Duke of York, Wellesley summed up his view at the time of the likely enemy intent:

> I thought it probable that if I did not attack the enemy, he would attack me; and I prepared for the conflict at daylight in the morning, by posting the 9-pounders, and strengthening my right, where I expected the attack, from the manner in which the enemy had patrolled towards that point in the line during the 19th and 20th.

In expectation of the enemy's intervention from the south up the Maceira Valley, three brigades were deployed on what would become known as the West Ridge, a steeply-sloped feature with its right flank firmly anchored on the coastline. Further inland beyond the Maceira Stream, up on Vimeiro Hill, Fane's brigade covered the left flank. The army's baggage and artillery park were assembled in the Maceira Valley to the north-west of the village of Vimeiro.

So protected, overnight on the 20th/21st, Acland's brigade arrived and as a part of Sir John Moore's abortive expedition to Sweden, they had been for the best part of three months onboard ship so were no doubt relieved to be ashore. By 0600 hours the brigade had marched inland and taken up position on the southern end of East Ridge overlooking Vimeiro. Anstruther's brigade marched to Vimeiro as soon as it landed.

Now with a strength of almost 17,000 men following the landing of most of the reinforcements, General Wellesley reorganized his eight brigades. For instance, the 50th Foot hitherto in Bowes' brigade joined Fane's. This battalion was in lieu of the aforementioned five companies of the 5th 60th Rifles that were redeployed to other brigades.

On the evening of the 20th, Wellesley received word that General Sir Harry Burrard had arrived in Maceira Bay aboard the sloop of war HMS *Brazen*. He was rowed out to the ship to report to the new commander and outlined his intentions to resume the march south. Burrard, however, with the expectation of the arrival of the rest of Sir John Moore's expedition, promptly forbade any resumption of the march on Lisbon, stating that the additional numbers would secure the force. The new senior officer did, however, allow Wellesley to retain command of the forthcoming battle.[9]

The Deployment of Piquets

While covering the landing of the reinforcement brigades, the forward infantry brigades deployed the normal piquets a mile to a mile and a half forward of the army. For example, the battalions of Fane's brigade contributed to a total of 200 men at a time to form the piquets, in this case under a field officer of the 50th Foot. Fane's outposts were deployed across the front of Vimeiro Hill 1½ miles forward covering routes including those through an extensive wooded area. On the night of 20/21 August, both Captain Leach and Rifleman Harris of the 2nd 95th were among those out with the piquets. Harris recalled:

> The night before the battle of Vimeiro, I was posted in a wood in the front of our army. As I peered into the thick wood around me I became aware of footsteps approaching and challenged in a low voice. Receiving no answer, I brought my rifle to the port and bade the strangers come forward. They were Major Napier, then of the 50th foot, and an officer of the Rifles.[10]
>
> The major came close up to me and looked hard in my face. 'Be alert here sentry for I expect the enemy upon us tonight, but I know not how soon.'

General Wellesley's initial deployment at dawn on 21 August 1808.

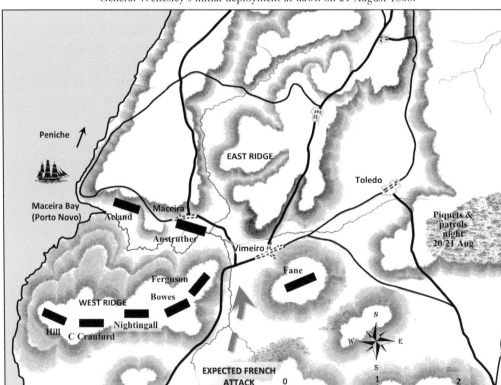

I was a young soldier then, and the lonely situation I was in, together with the impressive manner in which Major Napier delivered his caution, made a great impression on me.[11]

Deployed beyond the infantry piquets the 20th Light Dragoons provided a chain of vedettes about 3 miles south and east of the army. Wellesley, however, later drew attention to his lack of cavalry: 'My patrols gave me intelligence of movements by the enemy but as we were so very inferior in cavalry, my patrols could not go to any distance, and of course their reports were very vague, and not founded on very certain grounds.'

Over the previous days the French cavalry had served General Junot well. They had identified the southerly orientation of Wellesley deployment on the Western Ridge by 'three lines of campfires' belonging to Hill's, C. Craufurd's and Nightingall's brigades and that the southerly slope was steep. Consequently, choosing easier ground to the east of Vimeiro, Junot ordered his divisions to turn the British flank and attempt an envelopment, which if all went well would pin Wellesley's army on the coast as the first step of 'throwing them back into the sea'. Advancing against Vimeiro Hill were the two divisions of Loison and Delaborde. Attacking on the left of the hill, the former had both of his brigades, led by Chalot's. The former on the right was to attack the hill from the east, but consisted of just Thomières' brigade. Brenier's brigade was detached and would take a longer and wide loop to the east to envelop Wellesley's army. This march in a north-westerly direction would take Brenier to the crest of East Ridge near the village of Ventosa.

General Wellesley, having been ordered not to resume his advance south, on the evening of 20 August issued the following order in expectation of a French attack: 'Night Pass Order. The army will halt to-morrow. The men to sleep accoutred to-night, in readiness to turn out, and to be under arms at three o'clock in the morning.' Well before dawn, however, the cavalry patrols he had deployed warned him that the French were some 4 miles from the army, not to the south but to the south-east. Sergeant Landscheit was commanding one of the cavalry patrols and had been drawn well forward of the piquets provided by his regiment, the 20th Light Dragoons, by word from a local Portuguese that the French were on the march. This was soon confirmed by the sound in the still night of horses' hoofs and the heavy rumbling of wheels on a wooden bridge. He promptly returned with the first accurate information through the British cavalry and infantry piquets to report to General Fane:

There was much challenging, of course, as we drew towards the videttes [*sic*], and demanding and giving the countersign, for we rode briskly; and whether we came as friends or foes, our people knew that there must be something in the wind. Our protracted absence, too, had greatly alarmed

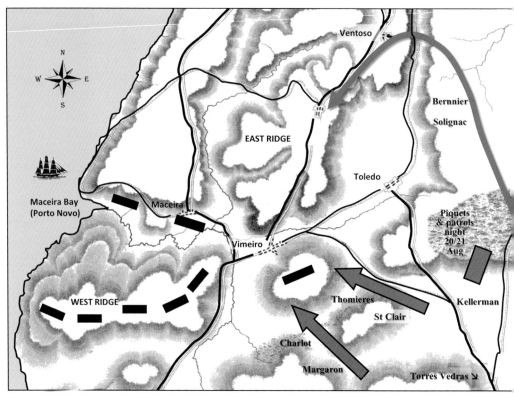

General Junot's plan of attack, 21 August 1808.

them; and General Fane himself, irritated by the state of suspense in which he had been kept, was at hand to bid us welcome. He opened upon me with a volley of abuse, such as I had rarely listened to before; and charged me with all sorts of military crimes, not the least prominent of which was stupidity. I permitted him to exhaust both his breath and his anger, and then told my tale. The effect was magical – I was now everything that was excellent; I was a true soldier and deserved to be rewarded. It was necessary, moreover, that Sir Arthur should be informed of a discovery so important, and there was no person so well qualified to convey this information as myself. Accordingly, General Fane desired me to ride immediately to headquarter-house, with the situation of which I was well acquainted, and to tell my story as I had told it to him, circumstantially and fully ...

I rode to the house where the general dwelt, and being admitted, I found him, with a large staff, all of them seated on a long table in the hall, back to back, and swinging their legs to and fro, like men on whose minds not the shadow of anxiety rested. Moreover, the general himself not only saw no consternation in my manner, but closely examined me as to the details of my adventure and told me that I had done my duty well. He then desired me to go below, and get something to eat and drink from his servant, which I did, though not till I had heard him give his orders, in a calm, clear, and cheerful voice. They were in substance these: 'Now, gentlemen, go to your stations; but let there be no noise made – no sounding of bugles or beating of drums. Get your men quietly under arms, and desire all the outposts to be on the alert.' This latter admonition, it is just to add, I had already conveyed to the outposts, warning each, as I passed it on my way home, of the enemy's approach; and the consequence was, that every man knew the ticklish nature of his position, and was prepared to do his duty, according as circumstances might require.[12]

With the approach of the enemy's columns orders were given for the army to stand to arms an hour before dawn, 'without drum or bugle'. The newly-

Troopers of the 20th Light Dragoons at a vedette.

arrived brigades were hastily deployed to strengthen the defences on the left flank, with Anstruther marching to Vimeiro Hill and Acland to a position on East Ridge overlooking the village of Vimeiro.

With the French having halted for breakfast at around 0900 hours, Captain Leach saw 'the enemy begin to appear on some hills in front, and shortly, some of their cavalry advanced towards the left of our army.' Following the cavalry 'several immense columns made their appearance towards the right and centre to take our guns, which were in the first line.' These were the

Lieutenant General Sir Harry Burrard.

brigades of Charlot and Thomières supported by Magaron's cavalry and a substantial battery of guns at Point 170 some 800 yards from the British on Vimeiro Hill. Leach continued:

> We remained in the wood until several men were killed and shots flew like hail, when the field officer of the pickets [*sic*] ordered us to retreat precipitately as our artillery dared not fire a shot at the French column (which were pressing hastily on) till we fell back.[13]

Leach described this as 'retreating firing' or 'fire and retire'. File pairs would work together, with one man firing and then withdrawing approximately twelve paces and loading. Once loaded, his partner would similarly fire, withdraw and load; the process being repeated until ordered to halt.

A diagram adapted from Cooper's 1807 manual for light infantry demonstrating the process of 'Fire and retire'.

The rear rank having fired and retired 24 paces and reloads. The process is repeated until ordered to 'halt' when the front rank closes onto the rear rank men.

Having retired and re-loaded the front rank man shouts 'Atkins loaded'. The rear rank man aims, fires and retires 24 paces.

Retiring twelve paces was standard but could be varied according to circumstances and the ground.

The skirmish line is ordered to 'Fire and retire'. The front rank man aims, fires and retires twelve paces. The rear rank man observes to his front.

Light dragoons wearing the pre-1812 uniform, with their regimental guidon.

Chapter Six

Junot's Attacks on Vimeiro Hill

Captain William Warre, one of General Ferguson's ADCs, had been awake on duty for much of the night of 20/21 August:

> About 8 I was woken by a serjeant, who told me our picquets of the 40th on the left were driven in and the enemy advancing. I ran to tell Genl. Ferguson, and we were soon on horseback and on the hill on the left, from whence we had a full view of the French Army, on its march to attack us in two strong columns. The strongest and principal attack was on our centre, and the other against the hill, and left of our position, which was separated from the centre by a deep valley covered with vineyards, occupied by our light troops, and to the top of which Genl. Ferguson ordered his brigade to advance to await their attack. Sir A. Wellesley arrived soon after, as I had been sent to tell him of the attack, and perceiving the intention of the enemy, ordered Genl. Bowes' and Genl. Acland's brigades to support Genl. Ferguson's; and made his dispositions in the most cool and masterly style, as from our commanding situation we could see all the movements of the French and of our own army.[1]

As the French closed on his army, Wellesley could see with clarity that Junot's attack was not going to fall on West Ridge but to the east and north, which would turn his left flank. To meet this threat he redeployed his brigades, less Hill's, from West Ridge, via the rear of Vimeiro onto East Ridge. Colonel Trant's Portuguese also marched north from Maceira, while Anstruther's and Fane's brigades remained holding the key Vimeiro Hill that was now right of Wellesley's centre. Fane's half-battery of light 6-pounders, now commanded by Captain Elliot, was reinforced by Colonel Robe's 9-pounder guns from the artillery reserve.[2] General Ferguson's and Bowes' brigades were also deployed north on to East Ridge to join the 40th Foot, which had been the sole occupiers of the waterless ridge. Brigadier Anstruther described the approach of the French:

> The enemy came rapidly along the road, directly in front of the 50th, and when within about 900 yards deployed to their left, so as to bring their front parallel to ours; heavy cannonade from our guns, which

caused the enemy much loss, but did not check his advance. Brigadier-General Fane sent out nearly all the 60th and some companies 95th, to skirmish with their sharpshooters; after a good deal of firing our people were driven in ...[3]

In the final stage of the retirement of the two British brigade's piquets, some of the guns, presumably the 6-pounders, supported by three companies of the 2nd 52nd Light Infantry of Anstruther's brigade were sent forward to help them break contact with the French skirmishers. Once the skirmish line was out of the guns' arc of fire and withdrawing to the ridge to re-form, at around 1000 hours, the 6- and 9-pounders were able to engage the advancing enemy, raking the French columns with shot and shell. Rifleman Harris witnessed

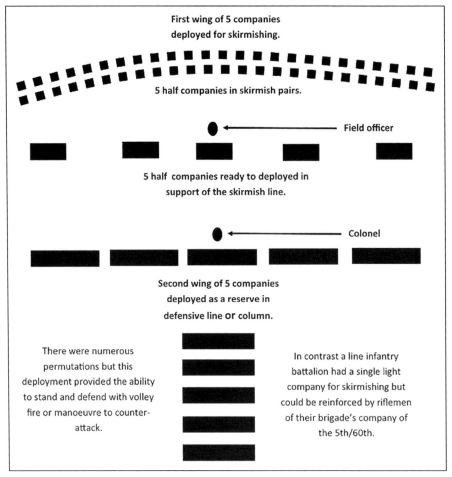

First wing of 5 companies deployed for skirmishing.

5 half companies in skirmish pairs.

Field officer

5 half companies ready to deployed in support of the skirmish line.

Colonel

Second wing of 5 companies deployed as a reserve in defensive line **or** column.

There were numerous permutations but this deployment provided the ability to stand and defend with volley fire or manoeuvre to counter-attack.

In contrast a line infantry battalion had a single light company for skirmishing but could be reinforced by riflemen of their brigade's company of the 5th/60th.

A diagram of a light infantry or a rifle battalion of two wings deployed for skirmishing.

the effect of their fire: 'I saw regular lanes torn through the French ranks as they advanced. They were immediately closed up again as they marched steadily on. Whenever we saw a round shot go through the mass, we raised a shout of delight.'

Harris was not just an onlooker of the developing battle:

I myself was very soon hotly engaged. Loading and firing away I became enveloped in the smoke I created ... The French, in great numbers, came steadily down upon us, and we pelted upon them a shower of leaden hail. Under any cover we could find we lay, firing one moment, and jumping up and running for it the next ...

Our feeling towards the enemy on that occasion was the north side of friendly for, greatly outnumbering our skirmishers, they had been firing upon us Rifles very sharply, as though inclined to drive us off the face of the earth. That day was the first time I particularly remarked the French lights and grenadiers who were, I think, the 70th. Our men seemed to know the grenadiers well. They were fine-looking young men with tremendous moustaches and were wearing red shoulder-knots. As they came swarming up, they rained upon us a perfect shower of balls, which we returned quite as sharply. Whenever one of them was knocked over, our men called out: 'There goes another of Boney's Invincibles!'

Colonel Torrens in his evidence at the Cintra Inquiry recalled Sir Arthur sending him 'with orders both to General Fane and General Anstruther, at the commencement of the battle':

Sir Arthur Wellesley desired me to ride as fast as I could to General Anstruther and to General Fane, and to convey to them his orders that

The view south-east from Vimeiro Hill to the woods in the distance where the piquets and vedettes were posted and the ground across which Fane's skirmishers retired at the beginning of the battle.

they should not move from the position which they occupied in front of the village of Vimeiro, without further directions from Sir Arthur. On my arrival at that position, I found that General Fane had advanced a little way in front and was engaged with some French light troops. I followed him, and delivered those orders, and he consequently retired: this was about half-past nine in the morning; but I cannot speak with any degree of accuracy.

As Fane's brigade retired to Vimeiro Hill, an indication of the impetuosity that got the Rifles in trouble at Óbidos is evident in Harris's account. 'As we fell back "retiring and firing" – galling them handsomely as we did so – our men cried out as with one voice, to charge.' Brigadier General Fane, however, was well in control of his brigade. '"Don't be too eager, men," he said, as coolly as if we were on the drill parade back in old England. "I don't want you to advance just yet."'

Captain Leach was later told of the fire effect of the riflemen during the skirmish action by a French officer:

> I met the English. Oh that morning was one of the most happy of my life! My men to a man had the same feeling. I was sent out to skirmish with some of those green-grasshoppers. I call them: you call them Rifle Men. They were behind every bush and stone and soon made sad havoc amongst my men, killing all the officers of my company and wounding myself without being able to do them any injury. This drove me nearly to distraction.

Meanwhile, Leach and the retiring piquets had rejoined the brigade that was centred on the 50th Foot which was positioned someway back from the south-westerly slope, enough to provide some protection from artillery fire.[4] He recalled that 'The business was beginning to assume a serious aspect':

> Some heavy masses of infantry, preceded by a swarm of light troops, were advancing with great resolution, and with loud cries of *'Vive l'Empereur!' 'En avant!'* &c. against the hill on which our brigade was posted. In spite of the deadly fire which several hundred riflemen kept up on them, they continued to press forward with great determination ...

Having driven in the British skirmish screen and climbed the hill and advanced through a small wood or olive grove 150 yards in front of the redcoat line, General Foy provides a view from the French perspective:

> The principal French column continued to proceed in its first direction. The position of Vimeiro wore a formidable aspect, because, between the lines of infantry,[5] amphitheatrically disposed and bristling with artillery, which covered the flat summit ... This imposing sight, however, did not

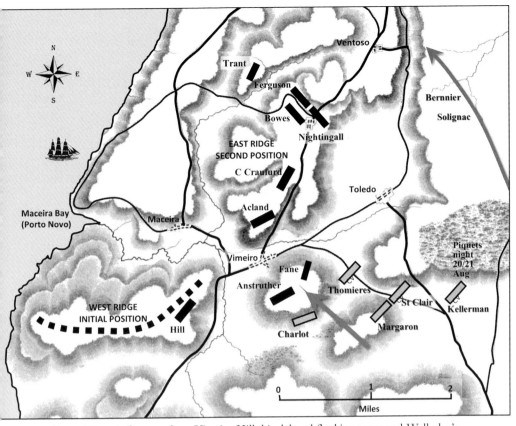

General Junot's first attack on Vimeiro Hill, his delayed flanking move and Wellesley's redeployment.

French line infantry prepare for battle.

stop General Delaborde, who, advancing against the enemy, at the head of the 86th regiment of Thomières' brigade, with a warm fire of cannon and sharpshooters, charged the 50th English regiment at the point of the bayonet. A few moments after, Generals Loison and Charlot brought the battalions of the 32nd and 82nd into action, against the 97th English, which was succoured by the 43rd and 52nd. In this attack, Adjutant-commandant Pillet and General Charlot were wounded. The Chief-of-battalion Peytavy, of the 82nd, fell pierced with wounds.

Captain Landmann of the Engineers acting as a staff officer had been sent to Vimeiro Hill in time to witness the French attack:

The 50th were in line, on the right of the reserve guns, and just sufficiently retired from the crest of the hill to be out of sight of the enemy; and instead of advancing in line, or by divisions or companies, to fire on the enemy, each man advanced singly when he had loaded, so as to see into the valley, and fired, on having taken his aim; he then fell back into his place to reload. By this management the enemy concluded that the guns were supported by a small number of Light Infantry only, and were manoeuvring at a long musket range, on some hills much inferior in height to those we occupied and making their arrangements for the attack.[6]

The French advance continued and Captain Leach noted that:

the old 50th regiment received them with a destructive volley, following it with a most brilliant and decisive charge with the bayonet, which broke and sent back, in utter dismay and confusion, and with great loss, this column, which a short time before was all confidence and exultation.

Having been only slightly engaged at Roliça, the 50th were in their first real battle and on the crest of Vimeiro Hill had been under French artillery fire for some time and latterly that of skirmishers. Captain Patterson later wrote:

Our men were at this time exposed in the open field, and scarcely knew from what direction the enemy were coming; but though they were nearly all young soldiers, unaccustomed to gunpowder, they behaved with a degree of steadiness worthy of their corps ... When the principal attack was made, and where the enemy, still pressing in, galled us with a peppering that was rapidly thinning the ranks, made our situation by no means either cool or comfortable.

Having stood under fire, it was now the 50th's turn to hit back at the enemy led by the 86th *Ligne* of Thomières' brigade:

The 50th regiment, commanded by Colonel George Townsend Walker, stood as firm as a rock, while a strong division ... continued to advance,

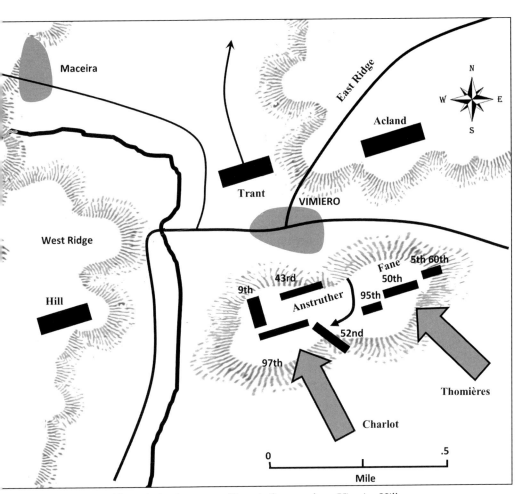

The culminating stage of Junot's first attack on Vimeiro Hill.

at a rapid step, from the deep woods in our front, covered by a legion of *tirailleurs*, who quickened their pace as they neared our line. Walker now ordered his men to prepare for close attack, and he watched with eagle eye the favourable moment for pouncing on the enemy.

When the latter, in a compact mass, arrived sufficiently up the hill, now bristled with bayonets, the black cuffs poured in a well-directed volley upon the dense array. Then, cheering loudly, and led on by its gallant chief, the whole regiment rushed forward to the charge, penetrated the formidable columns, and carried all before it. The confusion into which the panic-struck Frenchmen were thrown it would be difficult to express. No longer able to withstand the British steel, Laborde [*sic*] and his Invincibles made a headlong retreat, and never looked behind them till they reached the forest and vineyards in the rear.

To the right of Fane's brigade, Anstruther was equally successful. As Foy noted, Charlot's brigade fell on the 97th Foot on the crest of the hill who,

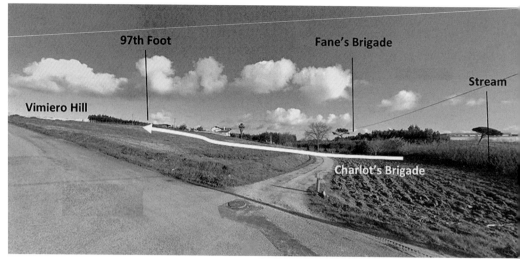

The ground across which Charlot's brigade advanced on Vimeiro Hill from the area of the stream at the foot of the feature.

according to Anstruther, 'were concealed behind a dip of the ground'. They were flanked by battalions of the 43rd and the 52nd Light Infantry, over-lapping the frontage of the columns of the 32nd and 82nd *Ligne*. Lieutenant Colonel Cameron, commanding the 9th Foot on the right flank of the hill, describes coming forward to fire from the reverse slope, with 'each company giving its fire as it came up to the crest line. The fire was kept up until the enemy had abandoned the wood.'

The 43rd's historian records that as the French advanced against the steady and motionless British line, 'they seemed to pause wondering why they had not been fired upon.' As they closed to within 50 yards, the lines of the 43rd and 97th made two sharp movements, 'Ready' and 'Present', which was

The 1806 Pattern shako plates of a centre company of the 32nd *Ligne* and the *voltigeurs* of the 82nd *Ligne*, both of Charlot's brigade.

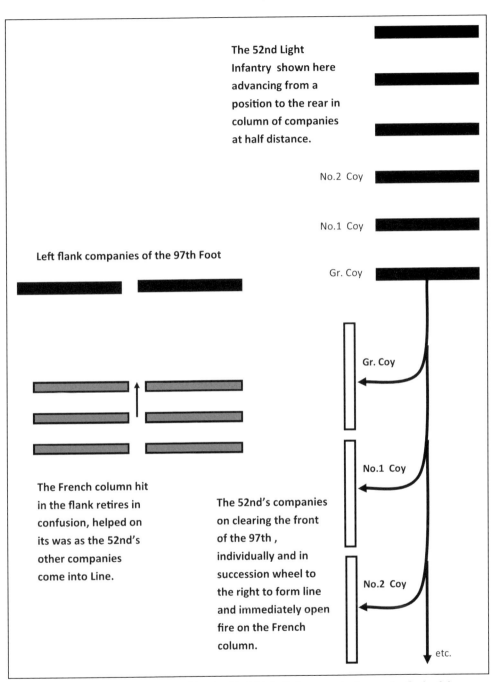

The most likely manoeuvre used by the 52nd Light Infantry to deploy on the flank of the French column.

followed by the order 'Fire!' and a devastating volley that swept away the heads of the columns. Through the billowing clouds of grey powder smoke the two battalions advanced, appearing with ported arms marching steadily forward. As the French reeled from the volley, the advance speeded up and with a bold 'huzzah' bayonets were lowered to the charge. At the same time the brigade's third battalion, the incomplete 52nd, was in action, probably consisting of no more than six companies. On the narrow confines of Vimeiro Hill they had been deployed in column of companies' echelon to the rear, without any French to their front. Anstruther ordered them forward at the double and they wheeled 'very dexterously' to the right and taking the shaken enemy column in the flank, completed its overthrow.[7]

The brigades of Charlot and Thomières both fell back in disorder pursued by the British infantry. Captain Warre noted that 'They made several attacks, and endeavoured to turn both flanks of the centre [on Vimeiro Hill], but were received on the left by the 97th, who charged them and drove them through a wood.'

Even though the first French attack had failed, this was not the end of the battle for the Vimeiro Hill and Wellesley's centre.

Junot's Second Attack

When Junot, from his post across the valley, saw that the attack by Charlot and Thomières on Vimeiro Hill had failed, he dispatched the two battalions of the 2nd Provisional Regiment of Grenadiers under Colonel St Clair to renew the assault. They marched west in column of platoons, 'along the woody height which descends in rapid slope on the right towards the ravine through which the road passes from Vimeiro to Toledo'. Foy noted that 'all the efforts of the English were directed against the grenadiers'. The Royal Artillery gunners fired shrapnel-shells, which

> at the first discharge struck down the files of a platoon, and then exploded in the platoon that followed. Their fire was feebly answered by the artillery of the first division and of the reserve, which was compelled to keep in motion, that it might not embarrass the march of the grena-diers. Notwithstanding this inferiority of support, and the loss which it sustained, the grenadier regiment pushed on till it came within a hundred yards of the flat summit. At the moment of its forming [line] for the attack, the column was assailed by the converging musketry-fire of six English regiments [*sic*, insufficient space, only Fane's brigade].

The French soldiers attacking in columns learned to hate the explosion of shrapnel shells above them and being struck by musket balls from above. They called shrapnel 'black rain' after the smoke of the black powder content of the shells.

Meanwhile, Captain Landmann was still on the left flank of Vimeiro Hill:

During the whole progress of this column, the artillery kept up a most destructive fire, each of the guns being loaded with a round shot, and over that a canister; and I could most distinctly perceive at every discharge that a complete lane was cut through the column from front to rear by the round shot, whilst the canister was committing dreadful carnage on the foremost ranks.

At this period, Lieutenant-Colonel Robe, commanding the artillery, and near whom I happened to be, turned to me and observed, 'You're a lucky fellow to be mounted, for my God! if something be not very quickly done, the enemy will, in a few minutes, have our guns and we shall all be bayonetted.' 'Then,' said I, 'order up your horse, and be ready for the worst.' 'No, no!' exclaimed the gallant Robe, with scorn, 'I'll neither leave my guns nor my gunners, I'll share the fate of my brave boys, be it what it may.' The words here recorded are verbatim those used by Robe in expressing his entire devotion to the service.

During this conversation the guns of the Artillery Reserve were still being served and General Foy describes their fire effect on the French: 'Almost all

Junot's second attack on Vimeiro Hill.

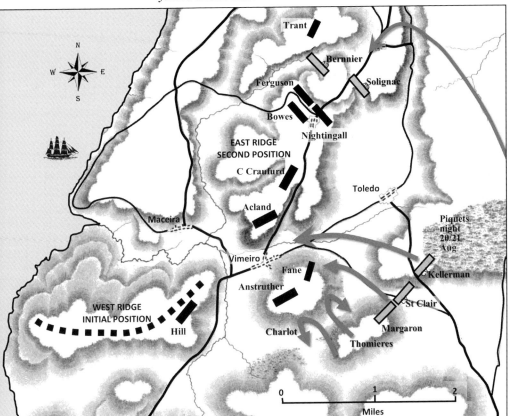

the horses of the artillery and the ammunition-waggons were killed. The Colonels-of-artillery, Prost and Foy, were wounded. The first two platoons of grenadiers disappeared, as if they had been annihilated; the regiment could not form line of battle in front …'

Landmann, on the left flank where the 50th Foot had been redeployed, continued:

> In this way, the enemy having very quickly approached the guns to within 60 or 70 yards, they halted, and endeavoured to deploy and form their line, under cover of the *Voltiguers* … Walker immediately advanced his gallant 50th to the crest of the hill, where he gave the words, 'Ready, present! and let every man fire when he has taken his aim.' This order was most strictly obeyed and produced a commencement of destruction and carnage which the enemy had not anticipated. Then Walker called out, raising his drawn sword and waving it high over his head, 'Three cheers and charge, my fine fellows!' and away went this gallant regiment, huzzaing all the time of their charge down the hill, before the French had recovered from their astonishment at discovering that the guns were not unprotected by infantry, as I afterwards was informed they had up to that instant fully believed.
>
> This rush forward was awfully grand; the enemy remained firm and almost motionless, until our men were within 10 to 20 yards from them; then discharged a confused and ill-directed fire from some of the front ranks, for the line had not yet been formed to its full extent, and the rear were already breaking up and partially running off. The whole now turned round and started off, every man throwing away his arms and accoutrements, as also his knapsack, cap, and, in short, everything that could have obstructed his utmost speed; and thus a gallant column, which but a very few minutes before this moment had numbered 5,000 [*sic*], at least, of the stoutest hearts in that army, was repulsed, scattered, and completely thrown out of action. The dispersion of this column presented a most interesting and curious sight; the whole of them being dressed in white linen greatcoats, gave them, whilst in confusion and running for their lives, exactly the appearance of an immense flock of sheep.

Foy, however, indicates that St Clair's grenadiers did not break and run but 'obliqueing to the right, in spite of the orders and example of the chiefs, it rushed headlong into the ravine'.[8]

An advance by St Clair's grenadiers into the 'ravine' alongside General Kellermann leading Colonel Maransin's 1st Regiment of Grenadiers took the French into the valley with a stream, the Ribiera de Toledo, which drains into the Rio Maceira and led to the village of Vimeiro. A successful advance here

Spherical Case or Shrapnel

During its limited role in the combat of Roliça, the British artillery fired their first few rounds of spherical case shot in anger, but Vimeiro was the first time it was used extensively.

Lieutenant Henry Shrapnel RA had served in North America, and on his return to England he experimented with combining two current forms of artillery ammunition: the howitzer shell and the canister (grapeshot) round. His idea was to fill hollow shells with lead balls and gunpowder that would be ignited by a simple time fuse to combine the effects of the lethality of canister and the range of shells.

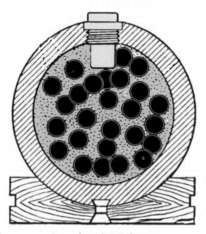

A cross-section of a spherical canister round.

He developed a relatively thin steel shell case that was sufficiently strong to survive firing but still burst with its limited powder content, which also propelled the musket balls down on the target. The difficulty was the accuracy of the fuse and the gunner's judgement of the range to the enemy.

Even though demonstrated in the 1780s, it was not until 1803 that the spherical case round was taken into service, but by 1808 rounds had been developed for the 6- and 9-pounder guns and the 5.5in howitzer. Arguably more effective than round shot, spherical case was able to take some of the effect of the limited range canister to engage the enemy at greater ranges. It also helped to make up for the paucity of guns in the British Peninsular Army, particularly when used against French columns which made good targets.[9]

would take the grenadiers behind Vimeiro Hill and of course would have turned Anstruther's and Fane's positions. Such an advance however, took the grenadiers across the front of Acland's brigade at the southern end of East Ridge.

Two of Fane's companies of the 95th were quickly redeployed to the left to fire down into the village and its approaches. Despite the fighting to his front,

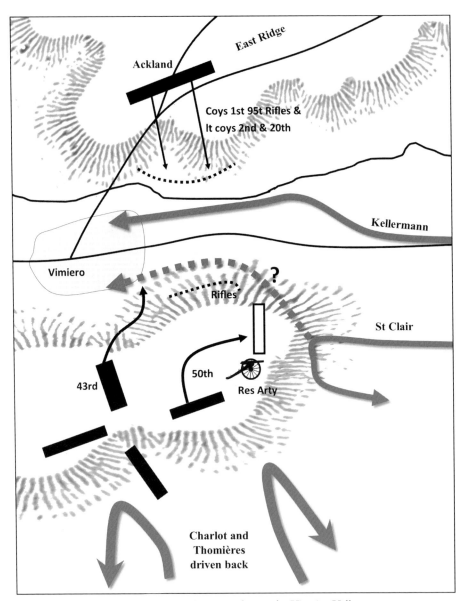

The French grenadiers' attack into the Vimeiro Valley.

General Anstruther sent a pair of companies from the 9th and 97th, along with two guns to his rear. While to the north of the village Acland deployed from East Ridge his two companies of 1st 95th Rifles, the light companies of the 2nd and 20th Foot and his two cannon. Thus, flanking fire from the north and south temporarily checked the elite grenadiers, who held their ground.

It took further intervention from Anstruther, who realized that a more substantial reinforcement was needed and dispatched the 43rd Light Infantry into the area of the cemetery. During the first attack this battalion had remained under fire, but not closely engaged in open column of companies to the right rear of Anstruther's brigade. Their historian recorded that

> When they [the 43rd] took up position, the assailants were literally within 5 yards under an embankment, and immediately directed a steady and destructive fire upon them. A desperate conflict then took place in some vineyards, the enemy pitching into the young battalion like mad, and many broken heads resulted on either side.
>
> Then, when the narrowness of the way and the sweep of the round shot was crushing and confounding the French ranks, the 43rd, rallying in one mass, went furiously down upon the very head of the column, and with a short but fierce struggle drove it back in confusion. In this fight the regiment suffered severely, and so close was the combat that Sergeant Patrick Armourer of the 43rd, and a French soldier were found dead, still grasping their muskets with the bayonets driven through each body from breast to back.
>
> The French immediately fell back along the whole front …[10]

Private Hamilton of the 43rd described the fighting:

> The enemy advanced on us with determination and valour, but after a desperate struggle on our part, were driven back with great slaughter. It was not only a hot day but a hot fight, and one of our men by the name

The view from the left of Fane's position across the Vimeiro Valley to East Ridge and Acland's position.

A portrait of an officer of the 43rd Light Infantry.

of McArthur having opened his mouth to catch a little fresh air, a bullet from the enemy at that moment entered his mouth oblique, which he never perceived until I told him that his neck was covered with blood. He, however, kept to the field until the battle was over.[11]

After much confused close-quarter fighting with bayonets amid the houses and walls of the village, the four grenadier battalions were driven from the Vimeiro Valley with heavy losses, but the 43rd suffered both grievously and disproportionately in the fight. They lost 6 officers and 113 men – almost a sixth of the 720 casualties for the whole battle.

Chapter Seven

The Attack on East Ridge and the Aftermath of Battle

While the fighting on Vimeiro Hill was under way, the French attack on East Ridge was developing. Ensign Leslie described the deployment of the 29th to reinforce the Left Wing under General Spencer:

> After gaining the ascent, the 29th, being the leading regiment, moved along the edge of the heights, which sloped abruptly to the valley below. After advancing some distance we were deployed into line. From this point we had a grand view of the country to our right below. We could distinctly observe every movement made either by our own right wing, which was posted partly in the town and along a rising ground to a wood on the extreme right, or those made by the enemy, then forming preparatory to their grand attack, while the light troops and riflemen were warmly engaged.[1]

The number of troops that Junot initially dispatched to undertake the wider envelopment was relatively small, namely Brenier's brigade that had fought only days before at Roliça, along with the cavalry of 3rd Provisional Dragoons Regiment. When Wellington realized that the weight of the French attack was developing to the east, he redeployed Caitlin Craufurd's and Nightingall's brigades to reinforce General Spencer's left wing on East Ridge. Junot must have realized his intent, and seeing Ferguson's battalions marching north-east along the ridge confirmed to him that Brenier would need reinforcement at the expense of his main attack. Consequently, before the fight on Vimeiro Hill was properly under way, Solignac's brigade of Loison's division had already been dispatched 2 miles north into difficult country that would force them to take longer than expected routes.

It can be argued that Brenier's presence threatening to envelop or cut off Wellesley's line of withdrawal had already succeeded in that it had drawn three brigades onto East Ridge away from Junot's chosen main effort on Vimeiro Hill. In the fight for Vimeiro Hill, however, Solignac's four battalions could have helped make a difference to the outcome. Not only that, but such was the distance, the fighting towards the northern end of East Ridge

109

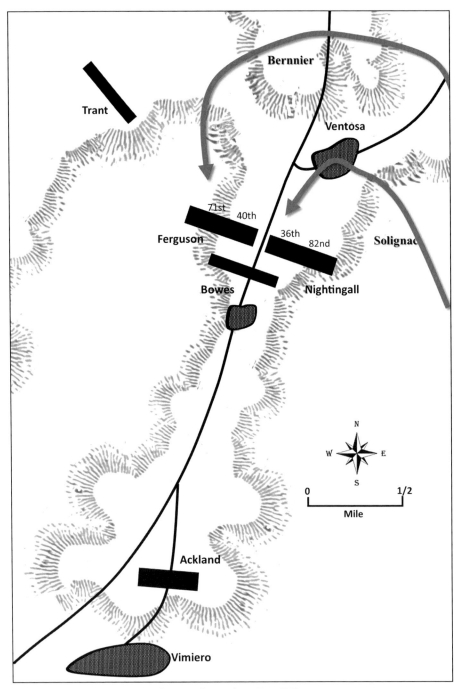

The French attack on East Ridge.

was a separate engagement and one that only began once the main effort on Vimeiro Hill had all but failed. In splitting his army, Junot stands accused of making a cardinal error.

Brenier had compounded the error when he came across a steep valley that lay across his line of march to the north-east of the village of Toledo. It being unsuitable for artillery, he swung in a time-consuming march well north of Ventoso at the head of the valley and turning in a westerly direction. Solignac, coming across the same obstacle, also turned north but not nearly as far as Brenier. Instead, he took the tracks via Ventoso across the valley, thus the two French brigades were separated and not able to act in concert. As the French crested the ridge, further down they saw the enemy.

The British with seven battalions from three brigades had been following the progress of a similar number of French troops. While the French were unsighted in some low ground they had deployed across East Ridge in line of battalions two deep and had lain down. Private Thomas Pococke of the 71st Foot of Ferguson's brigade noted 'We marched out 2 miles to meet the

General Brent Spencer, commander of the British left wing at Vimeiro.

enemy, formed line and lay under cover of a hill for about an hour.' Consequently, as Solignac reached the top of the ridge all he saw was the chain of British skirmishers and just behind them their formed supports. Possibly making the mistake other French commanders made when confronted by a thick screen of skirmish pairs of riflemen and light companies, he attacked thinking that this was the main enemy defensive line.

As usual the French artillery was in action first. Lieutenant George Wood of the 82nd Foot recalled the shot coming towards himself and a fellow subaltern:

> He was very near-sighted, and the French artillery playing on us at some distance, the unevenness of the ground made the balls come hopping similar to those bowled at cricket, which caused the men to open right and left to let them pass: at one of these openings this officer stood, and addressing himself to me, asked what was the matter? I replied, 'Do not you see what is coming?' at the same time giving him a hard pull. I was the means of saving him from that sudden death ... taking his quizzing-glass to his assistance, he gladly observed the ball pass and pitch 100 yards to the rear.

As the French approached, Ensign Leslie in Nightingall's brigade recalled that the next in action were the company of 5th 60th Rifles that had been newly attached to his brigade:

> In this battle the 60th Riflemen, who were all Germans, showed great tact in taking advantage of the ground and dexterity in the use of their arms. The General ... observing one of these men successfully hit one or two French officers who were gallantly exposing themselves in front leading on their men, exclaimed in the excitement of the moment, 'Well done, my fine fellow! I will give you half a doubloon for every other one you bring down.' The man coolly loaded again, fired, and hit another, then looking at the General, he said gravely, 'By Got, I vill make my vortune.'

The British reasonably expected that they would be attacked by the leading enemy brigade which was Brenier's, but as explained by Ensign Leslie that did not transpire. The first French in action was Solignac's brigade, which had taken the shorter route:

> It was a most inspiring sight to see the enemy advancing to attack. They were formed in two lines, the second supporting the front one. They moved with great rapidity and admirable regularity, pushing on in the most gallant and daring manner, apparently making a dash to force our centre. It had been thought that the first attack would have been made on

the left, where we were, and every preparation had been made accordingly. Sir Arthur Wellesley and General Spencer were riding through our ranks, but on their observing that the centre was attacked with such vivacity, their attention was turned to that point, particularly when it was found that a column of the enemy emerging from a wood was attempting to penetrate down the valley which separated our heights from the town and our right wing.[2]

Private James Todd of the 71st recorded that:

I felt my mind waver; a breathless sensation came over me. The silence was appalling. I looked alongst the line. It was enough to assure me. The steady, determined scowl of my companions assured my heart and gave me determination. How unlike the noisy advance of the French![3]

Lieutenant George Wood of the adjacent 82nd Foot provides a similar account of the French attack:

. . . a strong French regiment, which advanced to within half pistol-shot of us, when a most tremendous point-blank fire ensued. This not proving effectual, 'Charge!' was the word now vociferated from flank to centre: but, on their seeing us come to this awful position of destruction in the art of war, they had not courage to withstand our impetuous movement; for, just as we were in the act of crossing bayonets, to the right-about they went, in the quickest time. We followed as rapidly, driving them from their artillery – I believe, about twelve fieldpieces, passing it on the right flank at the same time the 71st Regiment did on the left, and I trust we had an equal share in the honour of capturing them.[4]

The view north-east up East Ridge and the French approach to the British position.

As witnessed by Ensign Leslie, there was clearly more manoeuvre necessary to beat off the French than described above, who had bravely advanced to very close quarters. Under pressure,

> He [Wellesley] immediately ordered the grenadier and another company of the 29th Regiment, whose right rested on the verge of the height commanding this valley, to retire to the rear, and brought up two or three pieces of artillery, which opened a well-directed fire. This, with the imposing attitude of our right companies, effectually checked the column of the enemy, who would have been exposed to a flank fire had they persisted in advancing. They went to the right about and retired in haste.

General Foy noted that 'three pieces of cannon were immediately taken, and three more afterwards, and a great number of officers and soldiers were killed or wounded. The troops were driven back into the valley of Toledo.' Meanwhile, as described by Todd, the British battalions re-formed: 'We advanced into a hollow and formed again; then returned in file, from the right in companies, to the rear. The French had retired to Ventoso.' Lieutenant Wood continued:

> The French, however, having now gained possession of the village on the heights, which had been strongly barricaded, remained there for the present, and we received orders to halt in the ravine. Indeed, a little breathing-time had become very necessary, as we had for the last two hours been firing, shouting, running, swearing, sweating, and huzzaing.

Piper Clarke, though wounded, placed the 71st into battle.

On the opposite flank, Brenier's brigade was coming into action closing in on the 71st. Private Todd recalled:

> We gave them one volley and three cheers – three distinct cheers. Then all was still and death. They came upon us, crying and shouting, to the very point of our bayonets. Our awful silence and determined advance they could not resist. They put about and fled without much resistance.

Todd concluded that 'The French came down upon us again. We gave them another specimen of a charge, as effectual as our first, and pursued them 3 miles.' During this second charge Piper Clarke was wounded, but sitting up as best he could he continued to play, with the skirl of the pipe urging his comrades on.

Foy describes the second attack from the French perspective in more detail:

> General Brenier's brigade was then forming in the rear and to the right of Solignac's brigade, towards the acclivity of Ventoso, where it was

General Antoine-François Brenier de Montmorand.

concealed from the English by the nature of the ground. It executed a change of front to the left. The thirtieth moved forward and fell unawares on the 71st and 82nd English regiments, which had halted in the bottom. The cannon were recovered. But, taking advantage of their enormous numerical superiority, the English returned to the charge in front, with six regiments of infantry, while Crawford's [*sic*] brigade arrived on the right, and began a fire of sharpshooters, which outflanked the French line. The artillery of the English also kept up a hot fire. The two parties came to close quarters, and the General was wounded and made prisoner. In vain the third regiment of dragoons attempted several charges; they were rendered abortive by the roughness of the ground, and many brave officers fell, among whom was the young Arrighi, allied hope of being victorious.

After the attack General Brenier, who had been seriously wounded in the leg, was found hiding in a clump of bushes probably hoping to be found and taken to the rear during a counter-attack. He was taken prisoner, but subsequently released. In a conversation with Wellesley shortly after his capture, Brenier enquired if the provisional grenadier regiments had been committed to battle, from which it was deduced that Junot had committed all his available troops.

Major General Ferguson.

By late morning, with both French brigades on East Ridge having been independently defeated, from the top of the East Ridge through their telescopes the French commanders were able to observe the turn of events around Vimeiro and 'marched off as only the French can do'. With Ferguson and the Left Wing pursuing and 'well advanced', Lieutenant Wood recalled the pursuit being halted and commented: 'Why we were not permitted to do more, when we had it in our power, I am at a loss to conjecture …'

The End of the Battle

The 20th Light Dragoons, numbering some 200 mounted men and the Portuguese cavalry mustering 250 sabres, had spent much of the two and a half hours of the battle in the valley beyond Vimeiro village and hill. Sergeant Landscheit recalled that his commanding officer, Lieutenant Colonel Taylor, repeatedly requested permission to charge as the fighting ebbed and flowed, only to be told that the time was not right. With St Clair's grenadiers supported by cavalry pressing the left flank of Vimeiro Hill, orders came:

> … at last General Fane rode up and exclaimed, 'Now, Twentieth! Now we want you. At them, my lads, and let them see what you are made of.'

Lieutenant Colonel Taylor, commanding officer of the 20th Light Dragoons, was killed at the end of the battle.

Then came the word, 'Threes about and forward'; and with the rapidity of thought we swept round the elbow of the hill, and the battle lay before us.

As we emerged up this slope, we were directed to form in half-squadrons, the 20th in the centre, the Portuguese cavalry on the flanks, and the brief space of time that was necessary to complete the formation enabled me to see over a wide extent of the field ... there were some infantry who had long and gallantly maintained the hill, but who were so over-matched, that our advance was ordered up for the purpose of relieving them; and never was purpose more effectually served. 'Now, 20th! Now!' shouted Sir Arthur, while his staff clapped their hands and gave us a cheer; the sound of which was still in our ears, when we put our horses to their speed. The Portuguese likewise pushed forward, but through the dust which entirely enveloped us, the enemy threw in a fire, which seemed to have the effect of paralysing altogether our handsome allies. Right and left they pulled up, as if by word of command, and we never saw more of them till the battle was over. But we went very differently to work. In an instant we were in the heart of the French cavalry, cutting and hacking, and upsetting men and horses in the most extraordinary manner possible, till they broke and fled in every direction, and then we fell upon the infantry. It was here that our gallant colonel met his fate. He rode that day a horse, which was so hot that not all his exertions would suffice to control it, and he was carried headlong upon the bayonets of the French infantry, a corporal of whom shot him through the heart.

As happened all too often with much of the British cavalry, as Landscheit confessed, the 20th were 'far too eager':

Though scattered, as always happens, by the shock of a charge, we still kept laying about us, till our white-leather breeches, our hands, arms, and swords, were all besmeared with blood. Moreover, as the enemy gave way, we continued to advance, amid a cloud of dust so thick, that to see beyond the distance of those immediately about yourself, was impossible. Thus, it was till we reached a low fence, through which several gaps had been made by the French to facilitate the movements of their cavalry; and we instantly leaped it. The operation cost some valuable lives; for about twenty or thirty of the French grenadiers had laid themselves on their bellies beneath it, and now received us as well as they could upon their bayonets. Several of our men and horses were stabbed, but of the enemy not a soul survived to speak of his exploit – we literally slew them all – and then, while in pursuit of the horse, rushed into an enclosure, where to a man we had well-nigh perished.

A senior French infantry officer.

Captain Patterson provides an onlooker's view of the charge:

While we were pursuing our opponents, the 20th Light Dragoons, led on by Colonel Taylor, galloped furiously past us, in order to put a finishing stroke to the business, by completing anything that the infantry might have left undone. The horsemen, unsupported, charging the enemy with impetuosity, and rashly going too far, were involved in a difficulty of which, in their eagerness to overtake the stragglers, they had never thought; for, getting entangled among the trees and vineyards, they could do but little service, and suffered a loss of nearly half their number: their brave commander being also one of those who fell in that desperate onset.[5]

In the aftermath of the 20th's cavalry action and with the French infantry falling back in confusion, Anstruther's and Fane's men followed them across the valley in front of them and captured the French guns on Point 170. Captain Patterson presents a flavour of the pursuit by the 50th Foot:

As far as the eye could reach over the well planted valley, and across the open country lying beyond the forest, the fugitives were running in wild disorder, their white sheep-skin knapsacks discernible among woods far distant. There were, however, many resolute fellows, who, in retiring, took cover behind the hedgerows, saluting us with parting volleys, which did considerable execution amongst our advancing troops. At length, even this remnant of the vanquished foe, dispersed and broken in piece-meal, betook themselves to flight in every quarter of the field. The ground was thickly strewed with muskets, side arms, bayonets, accoutre-ments, and well-filled knapsacks, all of which had been hastily flung away as dangerous incumbrances. Several of the packs contained various articles of plunder, including plate in many shapes and forms, which they had robbed from the unfortunate Portuguese.

French artillery officer Captain Hulot was struggling to extricate his guns through the chaos of fleeing infantrymen:

We tried in vain to stem the panic by falling back a short distance and occupying a small village that stood behind us. Barricading the main streets, I set my guns up to cover the few ways in, but such was the press that they were in several places overturned, while I myself was almost knocked down despite being on horseback.

With the French falling back in disorder from Vimeiro Hill and the top of East Ridge, they were only pursued by the British for a short distance, much to the surprise of Junot's officers. Rallying the fleeing infantry was aided by the belated arrival of two battalions from Lisbon around which the French troops were halted and reformed. By 1400 hours a defence of sorts was in place to cover the withdrawal to Torres Vedras.

General Burrard's Decision

By midday General Burrard been landed by HMS *Alfred*'s cutter and had ridden forward to take command, but the battle was all but over. Wellesley and his staff who had returned from East Ridge rode over to him and, conceding to his rank, said:

> Sir Harry now is your time to advance. The enemy are completely beaten, and we shall be in Lisbon in three days. We have a large body of troops which have not yet been in action; let us move them from the right on the road to Torres Vedras and I will follow the French with the left [towards Santarém].[6]

Captain Landmann, a senior Royal Engineer officer, was now back with Wellesley who was being instructed by Burrard to make a map of the battle for the dispatch:

> At this moment, Sir Arthur ... came up, and pressed Sir Harry to order General Hill to move on towards Lisbon, adding, that his division was quite fresh, since the men had dined whilst the first line had been

Lieutenant General Sir Arthur Wellesley.

fighting; that they had not marched one step more than to take up the position they then occupied, and had not fired a single shot during that day. Sir Arthur made some further observations about the advantages we possessed, arising from local circumstances and of momentary value only; but Sir Harry resisted every argument for advancing, by making some allusion to a conversation they had had on the preceding evening on board of the *Brazen*.

Captain Lord Burgash of the 3rd Dragoon Guards was also present and recalled that Wellesley had pointed out 'that he had four brigades that had not been engaged and that Torres Vedras was the pass by which the enemy must retire to Lisbon'. While this discussion was going on, a message arrived via an ADC from General Ferguson explaining that he had a body of French at a distinct disadvantage and wanted to continue. He later told the Cintra Inquiry that:

> A column of the enemy completely broken, and consisting, in my opinion, of from 1,500 to 2,000 men, had, in their confusion, gone into a hollow, and were thereby placed in a situation to have been cut off from their main body, by a movement in advance by the corps under my command.

General Burrard, however, stuck to his refusal to allow any further advance or action, despite Wellesley's assurances, as he still believed that Junot had fresh troops available and argued that he had insufficient cavalry. He also stated that Ferguson and Hill at 3 miles apart on opposite flanks were too far apart and the wounded needed attention. He obdurately reiterated his order that there was to be no advance, but the army would await the arrival of further brigades of Sir John Moore's reinforcements.

Wellesley reputedly returned to his staff and, with some laconic bitterness, said: 'Gentlemen, nothing now remains to be done but to go and shoot red-legged partridges.' According to Captain Landmann, to add insult to injury Burrard then

> inquired of Sir Arthur at what time his dinner would be ready, assuring us, as he tapped his full-sized waist two or three times with his open hand in a most inquisitive manner, that the sea air had very much sharpened his appetite.
>
> On perceiving that Sir Harry Burrard had determined on not following up our advantages, Sir Arthur Wellesley reined in his horse 4 or 5 yards, dropped the bridle on his horse's neck, pulled down his cocked hat to the bridge of his nose, and having folded his arms, he drooped his head, and remained during some minutes in that position, evidently regretting that he could not follow his own opinion.

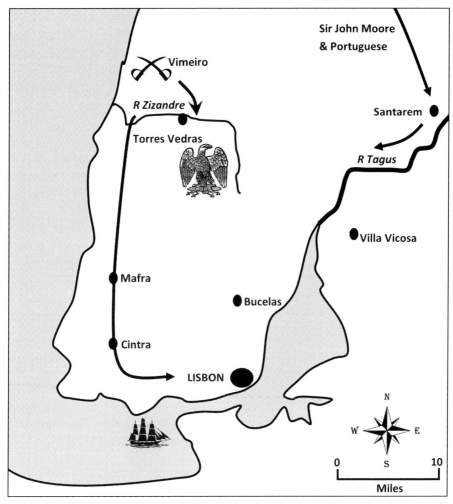

Wellesley's plan that was discarded by Burrard for the advance on Lisbon after the Battle of Vimeiro, outflanking Junot via Mafra and blocking his retreat at Santarém.

At the subsequent Cintra Inquiry Sir Harry read a narrative of his actions, as follows:

> About the close of the action, when it was evident that the enemy must be everywhere repulsed, Sir Arthur came up to me and proposed to advance. I understood he meant the movement to be from our right and towards Torres Vedras ... I answered that I saw no reason for altering my former resolution of not advancing, and as far as my recollection goes, I added that the same reasoning which before determined me to wait for the reinforcements had still its full force in my judgement and opinion.[7]

Aftermath

There was to be no pursuit of the defeated enemy and the brigades were ordered to halt and return to their bivouacs. As the soldiers retraced their steps and the hot blood of battle subsided, Lieutenant Wood of the 82nd Foot, having fought in his first battle, later reflected on his feelings and those of his fellow subaltern officers:

> When this day's fight was over, those who had escaped had congratulated each other on their good fortune. Amongst these was an officer who had his hat much shattered by the splinter of a shell, which a junior one perceiving, said 'Oh, my dear fellow, I am very sorry to see your hat so broken!' 'Thank you,' replied the other, 'but I suppose you would rather have seen my head, and then you would have risen a step.'
>
> We now returned to our former ground, and immediately fell to work making fires to boil our kettle; for, though the killed and wounded presented shocking sights on all sides, this did not take away our appetites: the more habitual a distressing scene becomes, the less it is regarded, till at length such sights are rendered familiar.
>
> We went to sleep on this bed of honour with as much unconcern as if it had been on soft and downy beds at home, hoping that the morning's dawn would lead us on to a rapid pursuit.

Searching for their dead and wounded occupied the 20th Light Dragoons. Sergeant Landscheit was one of those who volunteered to 'seek for Colonel Taylor's body':

> We moved to the front, Captain Bingham Newland of my troop being along with us, and found the declivity of the hill and the plain below covered with the killed and wounded. There they lay, English and French thrown promiscuously together, while hordes of peasants, together with women from our own army, were already in full occupation as plunderers ... We found Colonel Taylor stripped to the drawers, lying where he had fallen, upon his face.

Major Ross-Lewin of the 32nd had marched down from East Ridge with Bowes' brigade and went to have a look at the battlefield around Vimeiro:

> Upon entering the churchyard of the village of Vimiera [*sic*], my attention was arrested by very unpleasant objects – one, a large wooden dish filled with hands that had just been amputated – another, a heap of legs placed opposite. On one side of the entrance to the church lay a French surgeon, who had received a 6-pound shot in the body. The men, who had undergone amputation, were ranged round the interior of the building. In the morning they had rushed to the combat, full of ardour

and enthusiasm, and now they were stretched pale, bloody, and mangled on the cold flags, some writhing in agony, others fainting with loss of blood, and the spirits of many poor fellows among them making a last struggle to depart from their mutilated tenements.

There is no time more fit for reflection than an hour of calm succeeding the stormy moments of a great battle – no place more fit than such a spot as that on which I then stood. Amid the excitement of the fight, the din of arms, the absorbing desire of victory, the soldier sees with an unshrinking eye the blood of friend and foe poured out around him ... But when the thunder of the cannon has ceased, the roll of the musquetry has died away, the smoke has cleared off, and the trampling and shouts ... the mind becomes painfully aware of the horrors of a field of battle.

Meanwhile, as the French marched away from the battlefield, they spread the rumour that the British had been defeated, clearly believing that the nascent rebellion against them would break out if news of their defeat spread in the population.

There were no French regimental eagles captured at Vimeiro, but Captain Patterson recorded that his battalion took a trophy:

The 50th took a standard pole and box, which were borne by a serjeant between the battalion's colours, as a trophy, during the succeeding

A pair of British 4-pound cannon and limbers.

campaigns. The French, instead of colours, display a small brass eagle, screwed to a square box of the same metal, both of which were attached to a pole or staff. This eagle is seldom exhibited in the heat of action, the staff being carried as a rallying point, in the same way, and for the same object as our banners.

This box could be something unofficial carried in lieu of the eagle on the pole of a battalion's *fanion* minus its coloured flag. The battalions of Charlot's and Thomières' brigades were either 3rd or 4th battalions[8] and would not have carried eagles, which were the preserve of 1st battalions of a regiment. Instead, they had a distinctive coloured flag (red and blue for 3rd and 4th battalions). Contrary to regulations, these were often embroidered with regimental and battalion details plus battle honours, and, therefore, would have counted as a 'colour' if captured, so they were probably taken off the pole in battle.

Major General Hill, later commander of the 3rd Division, had remained on West Ridge throughout the battle, therefore his battalions were fresh and could have led the pursuit along with Craufurd's and Bowes' equally fresh brigades.

Chapter Eight

The Convention of Cintra and the French Evacuation

For the French under General Junot, on top of defeat, the wider situation of being isolated in Portugal with a full-blown insurrection across Spain denying them help from other French armies was unenviable. General Foy posed the questions that must have been at the forefront of Junot's mind: 'Under these disastrous circumstances, ought the army to try once more the fate of arms? If it ought, then how? If it could not, what course was to be pursued?' In addition to the isolation, Foy summed up the immediate problems faced by the French army:

> From the prisoners it was known that the English army was about to receive reinforcements, which would raise it to double its actual number. Other reports announced that the Portuguese army, under Bernardim Freire, had been for two days at Óbidos; that the corps of Bacellar was descending along the Tagus; that already the peasants of Beira, led by the monks of Monsanto, had entered Abrantes, and had murdered there some sick soldiers, and that Pepin de Bellisle, the commander, had been treacherously assassinated. The intelligence from Lisbon was likewise alarming.
>
> Opinions were unanimous on the three questions. Enough had been done for the honour of the army. The troops were now no longer able to keep the field. To give battle to such numerous enemies would be only leading the soldiers to the slaughter. Neither at Lisbon, nor in any other part of the kingdom were there strong points, prepared and provisioned in such a way as to render it practicable to wait for the arrival of succours from France, at some tardy and uncertain future period.[1]

Despite the protests of French soldiers and junior officers who were so accustomed to a tradition of victory, Junot's senior unwounded commanders all agreed that an armistice to negotiate an evacuation from Portugal was the only viable course open to them.

While the French were contemplating their courses of action, on 22 August General Sir Hew Dalrymple arrived from Gibraltar and landed in Maceira Bay, the third commander of British forces in twenty-four hours.[2] Dalrymple

127

was clearly 'prejudiced against any opinion' of the younger Wellesley from the outset. Colonel Torrens at the Cintra Inquiry gave an account of what happened:

> Arthur Wellesley told me, that upon the landing of Sir Hew Dalrymple, he had gone to him to represent to him the necessity of an advance, and that he stated his reasons for thinking it necessary. Sir Hew Dalrymple replied that he had just arrived, and was consequently unable to form any judgement upon the matter; upon which, an Officer of the Staff spoke apart to Sir Hew Dalrymple, and then followed Sir Arthur Wellesley, and told him, it was the desire of the Commander of the Forces that he should make preparations for the march of the army, and give what orders he thought necessary for it.

That officer of the staff was Lieutenant Colonel Murray. Despite being briefed on the favourable situation after Vimeiro, in a wilful demonstration of his authority, General Dalrymple decreed that the army would not march

Lieutenant General Sir Hew Dalrymple arrived in Maceira Bay to take command the day after the battle.

that day but on the following day, the 23rd, and then it would only make a modest move forward. In addition, Sir John Moore's division was ordered to re-embark and to sail down to Maceira Bay rather than march from Mondego Bay to Santarém as Wellesley had planned. This measure, which Dalrymple believed necessary to strengthen his army, would have given the French a clear week to prepare defences of the Lisbon Peninsula if they had wished to fight on. However, before his orders could be put into effect the situation changed again. Ensign Leslie of the 29th Foot was in the Maceira Valley inspecting captured French equipment when:

> we suddenly observed several men and officers running past us as if they were mad, shouting out, 'Stand to your arms! Stand to your arms! The French are advancing.'
>
> We, of course, started off to our camp in double time. There we found all the troops getting under arms. The whole were soon formed up, ready to meet any foe. We hastened to occupy the same positions on the heights which we had done during the battle the day before, and were all eagerly looking out for the enemy, but none could be discovered. After some delay we received orders to march back to our bivouac. It proved to have been a false alarm. This arose from a party [two squadrons] of French cavalry having approached our advanced guard bearing a flag of truce, and escorting General Kellermann, who was sent by Marshal [*sic*] Junot to propose an armistice.

General Dalrymple cordially received Kellermann, who had a basic knowledge of English, to discuss the written French proposal for an armistice. It is widely acknowledged that Kellermann's ability to 'get the army out of the mousetrap we are in' was more successful than Dalrymple's 'over-generous' negotiating stance. The talks that lasted several hours and included Burrard and Wellesley refined the proposals and terms for cessation of hostilities for forty-eight hours. The basic terms were as follows:

- That the French army should evacuate Portugal, and be conveyed by sea to France, with its artillery, arms and baggage.
- That the Portuguese, and the French established in Portugal, should not be molested for their political conduct, and that those who thought it proper to depart should be allowed a certain time to quit the country with their property.
- That the Russian fleet should remain in the port of Lisbon as in a neutral port, and that whenever it sailed, it should not be pursued till the expiration of the term fixed by maritime law.

These conditions were to serve as the basis of a definitive treaty, to be settled by the Generals-in-chief of the two armies and the British

General Kellermann proved to be an adroit negotiator, presenting terms that Dalrymple
was consistently minded to agree to.

admiral, till which time there was to be a suspension of arms: the [River]
Sizandro forming the line of demarcation between the two camps.

Wellesley, despite his reservations about the overall generosity and some of
the detail, was ordered by Dalrymple to sign the document. His reasons
detailed at the Cintra Inquiry were as follows:

> The feeling was that with French garrisons in a number of fortresses
> across Portugal and holding various Lisbon and Tagus forts, a contin-
> uance against them of military operations was thought to be counter-
> balanced by the advantage of getting the French out of Portugal without
> any further mischief to the country or the capital by that of getting

possession of the fortresses without the difficulty and tediousness of a siege in the winter and also by preventing the attempt of the French to retreat towards their forces in Spain.

In a letter to Lord Castlereagh on the 23rd he wrote:

> You will have heard that one of the consequences of our victory of the 21st has been an agreement to suspend hostilities between the French and us preparatory to the negotiation of a convention for the evacuation of Portugal by the French. Although my name is affixed to this instrument, I beg that you will not believe that I negotiated it, that I approve of it, or that I had any hand in wording it. It was negotiated by the General himself in my presence and that of Sir Harry Burrard; and after it had been drawn out by Kellermann himself, Sir Hew Dalrymple desired me to sign it ... I object to its verbiage; I object to an indefinite [subsequently agreed] suspension of hostilities.[3]

While agreeing that the armistice avoided further fighting, Wellesley continued to protest at the sundry faults embodied in the negotiations up to and including the final convention. He explained:

> In the course of that morning he [Dalrymple] sent for me again, and he showed me the report which Colonel Murray had made. I again recommended to him to put an end to the suspension of hostilities, on the ground of the Admiral's dissent, without entering into details, and to leave it to the French Commander in Chief to recommence the negotiation for the evacuation, if he should think proper. Sir Hew Dalrymple was, however, of a different opinion, and determined to communicate, through Colonel Murray, to the French Commander in Chief.

Dalrymple had, of course, to inform and/or seek agreement with the Portuguese commander *Marachal* Freire and his fellow British commander Admiral Sir Charles Cotton. Writing in his memoirs, Dalrymple recalled that

> On the 23rd, the army advanced to a new position, within the line of demarcation; and soon after my arrival at Ramalhall, I was visited by the Portuguese General Freire de Andrade.
> The General soon entered upon the subject of the treaty, and the whole proceedings of the day before, with which he seemed to be much offended; particularly, as he thought that he himself, and the *Government of Portugal* (for such he considered the Junta of Oporto to be), had been treated with disrespectful neglect.[4]

Having easily refuted the claims of Freire, whose division had taken only the smallest part in the campaign, the proposal to release the Russian fleet was for

The Portuguese field commander General Freire objected to the lack of consultation with himself and the Junta headed by the Bishop of Oporto.

Admiral Cotton a different matter. As allies of Napoleon the British squadron had blockaded the Russian ships in the Tagus for months, and Cotton was not prepared to see them slip away as if they were neutrals and he refused to accede to that article. Dalrymple resumed his account with more than a little retrospective generosity to his actions and spreading of blame!

Sir Charles Cotton having thus declined to sanction the Russian article in the basis, I conceived the armistice to be at an end, and determined on sending to announce the recommencement of hostilities at the end of forty-eight hours. In consequence, I sent Lieutenant-Colonel Murray to Lisbon, on the 25th, with a letter, informing General Junot of the Admiral's decision; but, at the same time, I gave authority to Lieutenant-Colonel Murray, should Junot manifest a wish to negotiate on the remaining articles of the former agreement (that respecting the Russian fleet being expunged) to enter upon such negotiation, and to conclude a Convention upon the terms specified in a paper of memoranda, which Sir Arthur Wellesley had previously drawn up. Lieutenant-Colonel Murray was further empowered to prolong the suspension of hostilities for a definite period, should the negotiation be entered into.

There was spirited if faux argument on the part of the French before agreeing that negotiation on the detail of the convention before negotiations could begin with Colonel Murray during the following days. Days later General Dalrymple ratified the full text of the slightly amended Convention of Cintra

Lieutenant Colonel Murray did much of the detailed work on the Convention, but was working under strict instructions from Dalrymple. Murray later became Wellington's quarter master general.

around midnight on 30/31 August. Burrard and Sir John Moore, who had arrived by that time, were among those who also added their signatures.[5]

Major General Beresford, who was by then in Lisbon, wrote to Wellesley summing up his feelings and those of the population of the city:

> I had been much surprised at what I had heard of the terms, yet I had not a conception, till I read them, that they could by words have been so unfavourable to our cause and to the general cause as they now appear to me. The people here of every class are enraged to the highest degree, and this treaty has lowered us much in their estimation, which, however little we may think of the people, it was not worth our while to lose.[6]

Just over two weeks later, a *Times* correspondent summed up the indignation felt at home over the generosity of the Convention:[7]

> The Convention of Lisbon [*sic*] still continues to make every tongue eloquent, and every heart bleed, in those parts of the island where the extraordinary gazette has found its way; and as we further learn, through-out the army of Portugal, whose labours have terminated so unsuccess-fully. The honour of the country has been sacrificed, its fairest hopes blasted, and the reputation of its arms tarnished, the resources of the enemy increased and concentrated, the plunder of our allies sanctioned ... One can feel, therefore, but little inclination to laugh at the authors of such wrongs. Who can think without tears of rage and bitterness of an English fleet at this moment employed in carrying home a well-appointed French army, along with their colours, arms, ammunition, baggage and plunder, in order to unite in a fresh expedition against the liberties and honour of Spain?

The March to Lisbon

On 23 August elements of the army moved forward to establish piquets on the Rio Sizandro, the demarcation line between the opposing armies for the duration of the armistice. The town of Torres Vedras was not to be occupied by the piquets of either the British or the French, but many of the diarists mention visiting the town once the population had decided that there was going to be no fighting. While negotiations were under way the British army remained in its bivouacs, during which time Lieutenant Wood and his fellow subalterns of the 82nd Foot built huts of green-leaved branches that offered 'slight protection'. However, they were not up to a summer deluge:

> We had enjoyed the blessings of a sound repose but little more than an hour, when we were awakened by the peals of thunder breaking over our heads; these became more loud and dreadful the nearer they approached, until the whole earth seemed to tremble. The thunder was accompanied

by vivid flashes of lightning, followed, in a few minutes, by the most impetuous torrents of rain. Our snug settlement in the ravine was very quickly covered with a rapid stream, in which, by the constant light of the electric fluid, we perceived all our loose articles of dress, the only part we had taken off, such as shoes, hats, sashes, belts, &c. all floating away, and we had great difficulty in saving them. So heavy did the rain fall that it ran down the boughs of our hut like as many small waterspouts pouring upon us; and we found it more eligible to stand out in the midst of it, than to remain in the occupation of the hut … As soon as the morn appeared and the rain had ceased, we dried ourselves by collecting all the huts together and setting them on fire.

Chasseurs à Cheval on the march. They were the most numerous type of French cavalry in Portugal during 1808, normally formed in provisional regiments from squadrons of different regiments.

Only once the Convention had been signed would the French withdraw by carefully defined stages to Lisbon. For the British, the final 30-mile march to the Portuguese capital began on 1 September. Two routes were used: the direct route via Torres Vedras and Monchique, and the longer coastal road via Mafra and Cintra. Captain Patterson recalled the march:

> As we passed through the towns and villages that lay in our course, the enthusiasm and delight evinced by the Portuguese, on seeing the English army, was unbounded. Joyful congratulations, and the exulting language of welcome, greeted us as we triumphantly moved along; and, wherever we appeared, the most cordial reception awaited us. In the soldiers of Britain they beheld friends and allies, who had come to deliver their country from the bondage of Napoleon, as well as of French subordinate tyranny and oppression. On this account, the sentiments they entertained towards us, were those of heartfelt gratitude. Those feelings were expressed with vehemence and fervour, not merely by a class or a faction, but by all ranks and ages among the people, who saluted us with loud and deafening huzzas, and with cries of '*viva los Inglese – viva, viva – viva los officiales! viva muytos annos!*' while, as we marched beneath their crowded windows, a shower of garlands, flowers, olive branches, laurels and other harmless missiles fell profusely upon us. Entering Lisbon from the north, the 29th, 40th, 50th and 79th regiments halted upon an elevated space of ground called the Campo St. Anna, where we lay undisturbed for some days. The inhabitants around entertained the officers in a most liberal manner, their anxious care being to anticipate all our wants and wishes. In the full enjoyment of the variety and amusement of the Capital our time passed rapidly away. Temptations and enticements were not wanting to allure us from the encampment, and pleasure in many shapes appeared on every side.[8]

It is worth noting that several diarists commented on the 'strength of the country' for defence, as they marched through the hills beyond the Rio Sizandro. Clearly this was not lost on Wellesley either, who the following year gave orders to Colonel Fletcher for construction of the lines of Torres Vedras.[9]

While the locals were friendly, the French soldiery was far less so. Rifleman Harris was in the ranks of the 2nd 95th and later recalled that 'Three days' march brought us without the walls of Lisbon, where we halted. Soon after, the tents came up and we encamped.' Shortly afterwards, accompanying Captain Leach and Lieutenant Cox, Harris was one of the first British soldiers into the city on a mission to procure leather with which to repair his company's badly worn shoes. However, his abrasive attitude to the many French

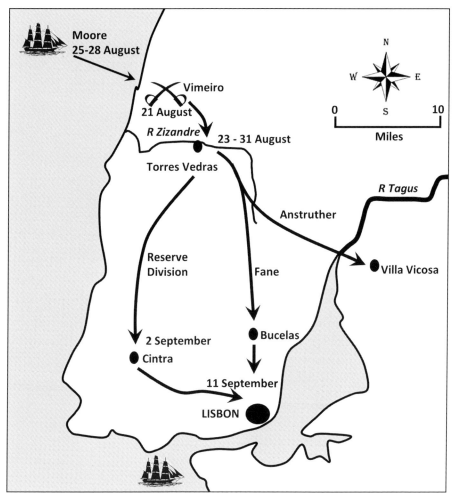

The march from Vimeiro to Lisbon.

soldiers residing there quickly got him into trouble (twice), firstly when spurning the offer of wine:

> I found myself in the midst of a large assemblage of French soldiers. Many were wounded; some had their arms hanging in scarfs and others were bandaged about the head and face. In short, half of them appeared to carry tokens of our bullets of a few days before.
>
> Although my appearance caused rather a sensation, they were inclined to be civil. Three or four rose from their seats, and with the swagger of Frenchmen, strutted up and offered to drink with me. I was young then and full of animosity against the enemy so prevalent with John Bull.

Harris was extracted by Captain Leach just as the situation was getting ugly. In his second encounter the French were less than friendly from the start and he was saved by a barman of a wine shop that he had unwisely visited. As British troops arrived in and around the city in larger numbers tensions eased, but even so there were incidents of fighting. As French numbers reduced, the British took on a protective role.

A major general wearing the plainer undress uniform.

The Evacuation and Loot

It took a full two weeks for the evacuation to take place, not least as some French garrisons such as Almeida on the border were a considerable distance from embarkation at Lisbon or Oporto. The embarkation of the first two of the three French divisions at wharfs in the city was covered by their third division which was protected in turn by the British, who had gradually taken over posts around the city from their erstwhile enemies. Captain Ross-Lewin, who commented on the dislike of the Convention across the army, added:

> The Portuguese were equally incensed, and with still greater reason; they had seen the French army march into their country without baggage; they had since seen them laden with the plunder of their towns, villages and churches; and they were now to see their despoilers, though beaten in the field and in most difficult circumstances, suffered to depart with their ill-gotten store, freely, and on board British ships; their allies were to provide means of transport for their enemies, with all their arms, horses and booty, to wish them *bon voyage*, to send them to amuse themselves at home as long as it should please them, and then to return and fight with renewed vigour on the same theatre of war. I myself have seen the large cases containing the plunder of the churches and dwellings of the Portuguese, as they were conveyed to the transports provided for the French, and some of them were so well filled as to require the united strength of eight men for their removal.[10]

The point that the French left Lisbon complete with their loot is regularly made, but one of the modifications to the treaty by Lieutenant General Sir Hew Dalrymple reads as follows:

> Art V is understood to apply to the baggage usually possessed by military officers and persons attached to the army as explained by General Kellermann in the negotiations for the agreement for the suspension of hostilities, property belonging to churches, monasteries and galleries of painting &c cannot be carried away. In respect to the security of purchasers of property it is a question of law in which the Commander in Chief cannot interfere.[11]

Later in the same document:

> No property belonging to any Portuguese or the subjects of any Power in alliance with Portugal at the time of the entry of the French army into that kingdom that has been confiscated on account of political opinions or under any other pretext shall be removed. It is also to be clearly understood that the stipulation in favour of persons carrying away their

private property is not to be made the groundwork of any commercial speculations.

These and other loopholes mentioning privately purchased property that can be found in the full text of the treaty in Appendix V made it impossible in practice to enforce the aim of preventing the carriage of stolen items. As a result, it is generally accepted that much loot was indeed taken back to France.

As the number of French soldiers reduced and the amount of the country's looted wealth that was being loaded onto British ships became more than obvious, tensions rose among the population and, according to Ensign Leslie, the French 'were eager for us to come and protect them. When we came to a French magazine of stores … we were received by the guard with all honours.' Ross-Lewin recalled that

While their effects were being removed, a case filled with church-plate burst asunder. The rage of the populace at this sight knew no bounds;

Commercial Square in the centre of Lisbon was one of several embarkation points for the French army.

they flew to arms, and would not suffer the French to embark, unless as prisoners of war; they also plundered the baggage of those troops, seized their arms, and would ultimately have taken away their lives, but for the great exertions made by the authorities and the British officers to prevent this last act of violence.

Despite taking over the citadel and putting in place 'precautionary measures', 'lest any serious tumult should be excited by the inflammatory appeals made to the public on the subject of the Convention', Ensign Leslie recorded that:

Three companies of the 29th Regiment were ordered to cover the embarkation of the French army. We marched from the Rocio to the small square in front of the naval arsenal and were drawn up in line opposite the grand entrance gateway, through which the French had to pass to get to the boats waiting at the wharf to convey them to the transports. Several columns defiled past us with music playing. After entering the dockyard they piled arms, each corps waiting till its turn came to embark. Many of their officers came out again and stood talking together. The populace, who had been in great agitation all the morning, on observing the French fast decreasing in numbers, and that we were now masters of Lisbon, became emboldened, and very audacious, reviling the French troops as they marched past, and shouting at the officers standing at the gate, calling them the most opprobrious names.

Military General Service Medals with bars for Roliça and Vimeiro that were finally issued to surviving veterans in 1848.

I heard a noise in rear of our line. On looking round, I observed about a dozen of French soldiers, officers' servants, carrying hatboxes, bundles, cloaks, &c. They were running for their lives, chased by a furious mob. Before I could get up to protect them a Portuguese lad drew one of the unfortunate men's swords from its scabbard at his side, and stabbed him to the heart before he had time to throw down the luggage he had in his hands so as to be able to protect himself. We, however, got all the others safe. Soon afterwards several artillery ammunition wagons, drawn by four horses each, came down the large, wide street, from the right, at full gallop. The mob, having attacked them by firing pistols and pelting them with stones, rushed out and drove back the outrageous assailants. But many of the poor drivers were seriously wounded, and one or two were felled to the ground.

With the French tricolour over the Citadel being struck and the final transports bearing the last of the 25,000 French soldiers sailing on 15 September, Lisbon echoed with *vivas* and the sound of celebration.[12] Despite the expectation of many during the long years of the war, the French never occupied Lisbon again.

Wellesley Departs for England

From the start General Dalrymple had treated the younger and junior Wellesley with resentment, no doubt fuelled by the Secretary of State for War's letter:

Permit me to recommend to your particular confidence Lieut. General Sir Arthur Wellesley. His high reputation in the service as an officer would in itself dispose you, I am persuaded, to select him for any service that required great prudence and temper, combined with much military experience.[13]

Consequently, Wellesley's advice had been regularly spurned but with the French having left Portugal, and with intervention in Spain being considered, he was tasked by General Dalrymple to travel to Madrid to conduct political and military liaison and negotiations. Wellesley replied on 10 September:

In order to be able to perform the important part allotted to him, this person should possess the confidence of those who employ him; and above all, in order that he may recommend; with authority, a plan to the Spaniards, he should be acquainted with those of his employers, the means by which they propose to carry them into execution, and those by which they intend to enable the Spanish nation to execute that which will be proposed to them.

I certainly cannot consider myself as possessing those advantages, personally, which would qualify me for the situation you have proposed for me; and you must be the best judge to instruct me, and are inclined to confide in me, to the extent which in my opinion will be necessary, in order to derive any general advantage from such a mission.[14]

Despite other such offers, with all that had passed since the Battle of Vimeiro and little prospect of commanding operations himself, Wellesley had already decided that he wished to go home on leave. This Dalrymple duly granted, and Wellesley, writing to Sir John Moore, made it plain that he was willing to serve under him. Sir Arthur sailed on 20 September, but not before the field officers who had served with him during the campaign had subscribed £1,000 for a piece of silver plate in appreciation.

Arriving in Plymouth on 4 October and reaching London on the 6th, Wellesley was soon made aware of the widespread discontent over the Convention of Cintra and that he was being held to blame alongside Dalrymple and Burrard. With Dalrymple being summoned home followed by Burrard, there was not to be any early return from leave to the Peninsula for Wellesley.

The Cintra Inquiry

With news of Roliça and Vimeiro along with the Spanish success at Bailén, the British population as a whole held high expectations of an unqualified victory over the French in Portugal. When word arrived of the terms of the Convention, after almost two weeks of silence from General Dalrymple, there was outrage among politicians and people of all classes and walks of life. Criticism was excoriating and pamphlets and cartoons ridiculed the trio of generals as was only possible in Georgian Britain. Criticism was not only confined to the civilian population. Major Bevan of the 28th Foot expressed the opinion that 'Sir Hew, if he had a military feeling, would have shot himself', while others not advocating such an extreme course of action were heavily critical. An added factor for Sir Arthur was the unpopularity of the Tory Wellesley family among Whig opposition politicians and supporters. Cintra was grist to their mill that was too good to ignore. With Dalrymple having arrived home, pressure grew for an inquiry into the Convention of Cintra. Eventually at the end of October the king acceded.

The inquiry into the Convention was held in the Great Hall of the Royal Hospital Chelsea between 14 November and 22 December 1808. The board of seven senior generals was presided over by General Sir David Dundas. After five weeks of poring over the details of the conduct of the campaign, Generals Dalrymple, Burrard and Wellesley were exonerated by the inquiry. Having concentrated on the purely military aspects of the campaign, the board was, however, promptly ordered to reconsider the over-generous terms

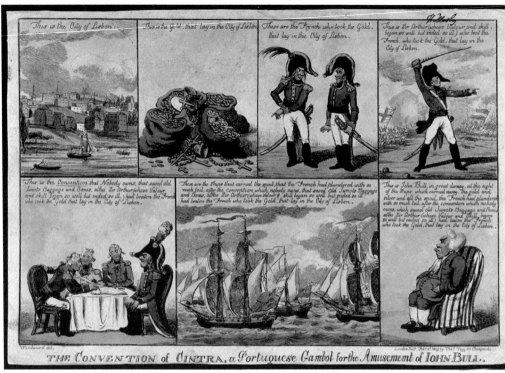

One of the many cartoons critical of the Convention of Cintra entitled 'A Portuguese Gambol for the Amusement of John Bull'.

The Great Hall of the Royal Hospital Chelsea where the Board of Inquiry sat.

of the Convention. Having reported back, five days later Dalrymple received a formal censure from the government and he and Burrard never received another active command. However, Wellesley's objections to the terms of the armistice that he was ordered to sign on 23 August as well as the final draft of the Convention on 30 August were recognized and he remained exonerated. Not only that, on 27 January 1809, Parliament voted their thanks to Wellesley for the victory at Vimeiro. This was a fair outcome, but it certainly did not stifle criticism of 'the haughty Wellesley' among his many opponents, but as far as Horse Guards and the government were concerned, he was exonerated in full.

Powdered and Queued Hair

During the summer of 1808 the steady change in the British soldier's look that had been under way since the turn of the century took another significant step forward with short hair becoming the ubiquitous norm. Captain Dobbs of the 1st 52nd Light Infantry, having landed at Maceira Bay on 22 August, was informed that the eighteenth-century practice of dressing soldiers' hair had been finally banned by an order from Horse Guards. He recalled a conversation that evening:[15]

> To the great joy of the men, they were relieved from hair-tying which was a burden grievous to be borne. And our huts being close to those occupied by the men, we could hear them joking one another on the subject; one of the principal ones was calling on their comrade to tie them, which was impossible, as their hair was gone.[16]

The dressing of hair, powdering and tying into a queue or club had been a part of military life for most of the eighteenth century, reflecting the civilian fashion of the day. As a practice in the army, it had been waning since 1796 when the first order was given for dressing to be abolished. However, as Captain Ross Lewin of the 32nd noted, 'So wedded do many persons become to old customs that some corps were to be seen dressed in this manner in '97 and indeed up to 1808.[17] As an example, Lieutenant Colonel Lake was killed at Roliça not only in a new uniform, but with his hair dressed and clubbed as of old, 'dressed like a gentleman'.

Ross Lewin continued, describing the tyranny of tying hair:

> When I joined in 1793, all military men wore their hair clubbed, that is, each had a huge false tail attached by means of a string that passed round the upper part of his head, and over it the hair was combed and well thickened with powder or flour; a plastering of pomatum or grease was then laid on; a square bag of sand was next placed at the extremity of the tail, rolled up with the assistance of a small oblong iron until it touched the head, and tied with a leathern thong and rosette so as to confine it in a proper position. After the arrangement of the tail, the officers' foretops were rubbed up with a stick of hard pomatum – a most painful operation, especially on cold mornings, and often calling the 'salt rheum' to the eyes; when this was over, the *friseur* retired

An example of powdered, dressed and clubbed hair from the second half of the eighteenth century.

a pace or two for the purpose of frosting, which was effected by means of an elastic cylinder, filled with powder, and so constructed as to expel, and let fall upon the hair, a light shower of it; and lastly the powder-knife prepared the head for parade, by arching the temples and shaping the whiskers to a point. In this agreeable manner half an hour of every morning was consumed. The men powdered only on 'dress-days', as Sundays, Thursdays and days of duty were called. Each dressed his comrade's hair, so that an hour was lost in dressing and being dressed.

To cut hair and abandon a long-held practice was not an easy decision for some, such as for Captain Landmann of the Royal Engineers:

It now occurred to me that my long queue might be inconvenient on service; so, after very serious consideration, I resolved on cutting it off, for it was my own natural hair and it hung most gracefully so low down on my back that I frequently tied it accidentally under my sash, but in point of thickness did not exceed that of a tobacco-pipe. Then were very few officers of the army who had needed so much fortitude, for almost all, to a man, wore false tails.[18]

Chapter Nine

Portugal between the 1808 and 1809 Campaigns

With Junot's army returned to France and General Dupont's defeat at Bailén, events in the Peninsula had decisively turned against the French 1808 invasion. The questions were firstly would the Spanish and their new ally Britain be able to profit from the situation, and would the balance in Central Europe established by Napoleon's victories between 1805 and 1807 hold? The key question here was would the reluctant and fearful vassal states and Russia remain aligned with France against a resurgent and vengeful Austria that smarted from the defeats at Ulm and Austerlitz? The conference at Erfurt confirmed that Napoleon would be able to take troops from the Rhine and lead an army of 250,000 to Iberia, where he would settle the affront to his imperial dignity once and for all. Not only that, but the British army, 'the Leopard', would be 'thrown back into the sea'.

The Spanish, buoyed to an unreasonable extent by King Joseph's with-drawal from Madrid to the Rio Ebro after barely a week in his new capital city, General Castaños' victory at Bailén and events in Catalonia, failed to act against the weakened French occupation in a timely manner. The Central Junta that had been established in Madrid lacked authority, and the regional juntas were mindful of their own defence. Castaños was not as expected appointed as *generalissimo*, and consequently the Spanish armies operated without proper coordination as they slowly advanced to exposed positions facing the French on the Ebro.

Meanwhile, with receipt of the news of victory at Vimeiro, Lord Castle-reagh wrote to General Dalrymple on 2 September, giving him the govern-ment's authority to march in support of the Spanish without further reference to London. This decision was based not just on British success in the field but on exaggerated reports from Spain, some simply over-optimistic and some designed to garner support beyond money and arms.

When Castlereagh's order was received from London, Dalrymple was still overseeing the evacuation of the French but had dispatched two brigades to the Spanish border, not for offensive purposes but to oversee the withdrawal of French garrisons from Almeida and Elvas. His preparations for operations in Spain were hampered by two factors: an almost complete reliance on the

General Francisco Javier Castaños, 1st Duke of Bailén.

Portuguese and Spanish for information on the suitability of roads for artillery and wagons, and a lack of detailed orders from London, without which he was reluctant to act.

The issue of maps and roads was one that plagued the British throughout the early Peninsular campaigns. The few maps that existed were inaccurate, and the Portuguese and Spanish engineers knew little of the geography and roads of their own countries and were of scant help. The process of dispatching British officers to produce itineraries of routes (places, distances, times, general direction and resources to be found en route) was only slowly begun.[1] To be fair to Dalrymple, knowledge of a host country's roads could have been reasonably expected, but his failure to make logistic preparations is far less excusable.

The politically outspoken Lieutenant General Sir John Moore was out of favour with the Portland government, but on the return of his abortive Swedish expedition he was dispatched to the Peninsula in an insultingly low position of third in command. However, with the recall of Dalrymple to London and receipt of a dispatch on 6 October 1808, Sir John found himself elevated to command of the army in the Peninsula. Of this turn of events, he observed 'How they came to pitch upon me I cannot say, for they have given

Lieutenant General Sir John Moore.

sufficient proof of not being partial to me.' With Portugal liberated from the French, Sir John received his orders from the Secretary of State for War:

> His Majesty having determined to employ a corps of his troops of not less than 30,000 infantry and 5,000 cavalry in the north of Spain, to co-operate with the Spanish armies in the expulsion of the French from that kingdom, has been pleased to entrust to you the command in chief of His forces.[2]

The specifics were equally vague and dismissed by Moore as 'a sort of gibberish': '... take the necessary measures for opening a communication with the Spanish authorities for the purpose of framing the plan of campaign, on which it may be advisable that the respective armies should act in concert.'

The British had liberated Portugal with a relatively small army numbering 17,000 at Vimeiro in a short campaign over little distance and with supplies from the Royal Navy,[3] but what was now proposed was that a substantial army would advance a considerable distance into the Asturias and Galicia regions of northern Spain. Sir John soon found that little had been done in preparation and commented that 'They talked of going into Spain as if going into Hyde Park.' With the army's operations for many years confined to small-scale expeditions, they had little practical experience of conducting a campaign over the distances and scale now envisaged.

Unsurprisingly, the most problematic of the army's departments was the Treasury-controlled commissariat, about which Moore said that 'a knowledge of their duties in the field was almost entirely lacking.' Resources were another problem; without a decent military chest Moore could not purchase the army's necessities, even if they had been available in the quantity required. On 9 October, in reply to his orders, he complained to Lord Castlereagh that 'The army is without equipment of any kind, either for the carriage of light baggage of regiments, artillery stores, commissariat stores, or other appendages of an army and not a magazine is formed in any of the routes by which we are to march.'[4]

Working sixteen hours a day, Sir John made progress in preparing to take the field and advance into Spain. The original plan was to march to join the left wing of the Spanish armies facing the French on the Rio Ebro. The majority of the army set out east over a period of two weeks during October by various routes to reassemble at Salamanca. Thanks to faulty information on the universally execrable Portuguese and Spanish roads and increasingly bad autumn weather, the march to Salamanca was time-consuming and the army was only assembled between mid-November and into December. Here with news of French reinforcement and the arrival of Napoleon, Sir John Moore remained undecided for two weeks whether to advance to join the Spanish armies or to retire back to Portugal.

In the meantime, in Portugal, until such time as the army had reached the Asturias and Galicia, the British operating base would remain at Lisbon before, courtesy of the Royal Navy, transferring to A Coruña. The small garrison was left in Portugal initially under General Burrard, consisting of ten infantry battalions and four squadrons of cavalry split between Lisbon and the border fortresses of Almeida (1st 45th and 97th Foot) and Elvas (1st 40th). This garrison was adequate while Sir John Moore's army was no further north than Salamanca and still covering the approaches to the frontier from the east.

At the end of October Burrard was recalled home to attend the Cintra Inquiry, leaving Brigadier General R. Stewart in temporary command before he in turn was replaced by Lieutenant General Sir John Cradock, who arrived in Oporto on 9 December 1808 and at Lisbon on the 14th. Ensign Leslie was with one of those ten battalions initially left behind in garrison:

> The 29th Regiment, owing to the severe loss it had sustained in the actions in which it had been engaged, and many wounded and sick still remaining in hospital, was, to our great mortification, ordered to remain in Portugal, and to be stationed in Lisbon. They consequently marched into the citadel.[5]

An outline of Sir John Moore's march into Spain.

The Loyal Lusitania Legion

The Lusitania Legion had been formed at the behest of Lord Canning, the Portuguese Ambassador and the Bishop of Oporto, under Lieutenant Colonel Wilson, in order to provide an organized military force to fill the vacuum left by disbandment and appropriation of the Portuguese regular army by the French.[6] Wilson was placed at the head of a group of Portuguese *émigré* officers who had fled Junot's invasion in 1807, along with some enterprising British officers. Having assembled in Plymouth, they landed at Oporto in August 1808 and immediately began recruiting, but patriotic volunteers quickly outstripped the clothing and equipment available.

Colonel Sir Robert Wilson as a general officer in 1818.

The green-uniformed Legion was organized and equipped as light infantry and consisted of three infantry battalions, a cavalry detachment of 300 and an artillery battery of four 6-pounders and two howitzers. The first group to be trained numbered 2,000 men. They displayed their quickly instilled discipline when they joined the British 6th Foot in helping to secure the march of the French garrison of Almeida to Oporto, where they protected them from the vengeful population during embarkation.

The Braganza green uniform of the Legion was of British design and manufacture, being a cross between Portuguese, British line and Rifles styles.

By autumn Wilson was complaining that he was in danger of becoming the private bodyguard of the Bishop of Oporto and needed an operational role. With elements of the British garrison of Portugal being stripped away to join Sir John Moore, replacing Anstruther's brigade in the border fortress of Almeida proved to be fortuitous. Away from the distractions of Oporto, Wilson and his officers could continue to train the soldiers of the Legion into a small but effective force.

Retreat

With no useful communication from Sir John Moore, General Cradock realized that the army had eventually marched north and feared that the battalions at Elvas were out on a limb and vulnerable. Consequently, he gave instructions to that garrison to head north, either to join the brigade from Almeida in a march to join the army or, if impossible, to take the road to Vigo. Cradock's intent when threatened was that the rest of the garrison would embark for Vigo or A Coruña. The Lusitania Legion remained at Almeida.

Meanwhile, Napoleon had entered Spain and secured Madrid for his brother Joseph on 4 December. The emperor deployed his divisions to protect the city, but failed to dispatch patrols, in an increasingly hostile country, to seek out the British. He had assumed that they had withdrawn to Lisbon, as indeed Sir John had contemplated for want of help and co-operation by the Spanish authorities, which it was noted were 'at odds with the zeal of the population'. However, realizing that 'the Leopard' was still within striking distance of destruction by his army, Napoleon put all other plans for a wider conquest of Iberia on hold. In full winter conditions, if anything worse than his crossing of the Alps, Napoleon directed all available troops across the Sierra de Guadarrama to catch Sir John's army as it marched on the isolated Marshal Soult in the province of León. Warned just in time to avoid Napoleon's trap and with the enemy just 60 miles north, Moore had little option but, as he put it, to 'run for it'. Captain George Napier, one of his ADCs, wrote:

> The instant Sir John Moore had read this letter he saw there was no time to be lost, as Napoleon would be on his rear and cut off his retreat through Galicia, and that a battle and victory over Soult could be of no advantage but most probably be the cause of the total destruction of the army by the immense numbers of the enemy in front and rear who were pouring down on our small force from all directions. He immediately ordered the troops to counter-march, and we commenced our memorable retreat to Coruña.[7]

The one advantage of the ill-founded advance into Spain was, as Sir John Moore conceded in a letter to the Spanish General la Romana, 'My movement has, in some degree, answered its object, as it has drawn the enemy from

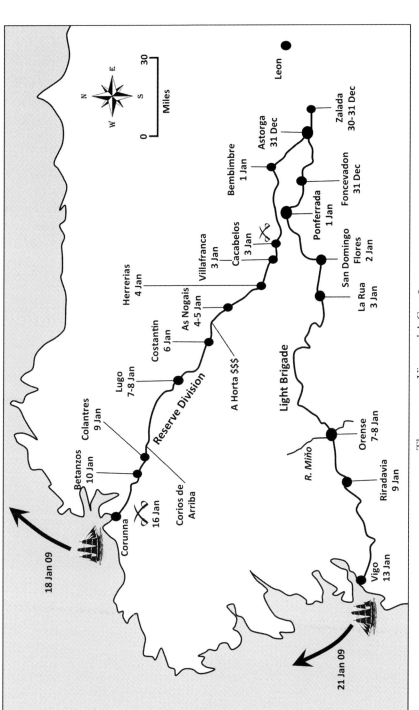

The retreat to Vigo and A Coruña.

Lieutenant General Sir John Cradock.

other projects and will give the south more time to prepare. With a force such as mine I cannot pretend to do no more.'

With the British army having escaped Napoleon's trap, evidence of domestic plots and relations with Austria heading for renewed war, the emperor left Astorga on 1 January 1809. He travelled to Paris at speed followed by his Imperial Guard, along with two infantry divisions and a pair of cavalry divisions. The pursuit to A Coruña was left to Marshals Soult and

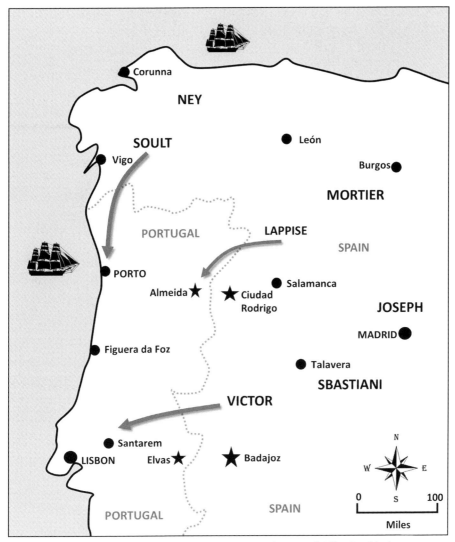

Napoleon's concept of operations for the invasion of Portugal following his departure from the Peninsula.

Ney, but despite the transports being delayed at Vigo by contrary winds, Sir John Moore's army was able to start embarking and defeat the French before slipping away. Sir John Moore, however, died of wounds.

Despite Napoleon's departure with a part of the army, a considerable number of French troops remained in an increasingly rebellious Spain. With orders to complete the subjugation of the Peninsula, the marshals were under-resourced and, without Napoleon's direction, largely looked to their own interests. Soult had been given orders to advance into Portugal from the north, while Marshal Victor with I Corps in the Tagus Valley was fixed, in his case by General Cuesta's Army of Extremadura. Typical of Spanish armies, though repeatedly beaten or driven back, it was never destroyed and never gave up the fight. Consequently, there was no immediate threat to Lisbon and Sir John Cradock was able to remain concentrated around the city.

At the end of December Admiral Berkeley delivered a dispatch to Lisbon from Castlereagh written on Christmas Eve. This, like other operational orders issued by Castlereagh, was far from clear and represented a change of direction. It briefed Cradock that, although some British units were to be left behind to assist the Portuguese, the field army was to be re-embarked and employed elsewhere in the Peninsula 'where most advantageous to the common cause'. This was probably to be further south, based in Cádiz. In the meantime, garrison troops were to be deployed within reach of Lisbon (Sacavém, just north of the city, and Santarém) and, if the French advanced in significant force, they were to be embarked on the ships of the Royal Navy.

During the retreat to A Coruña and Cradock's withdrawal of the border garrisons to Lisbon, Wilson and the Lusitanian Legion refused to conform and abandon Almeida. Instead, he decided, with the Legion numbering fewer than 2,000 men, to face the 9,000-strong French division commanded by General Lapisse, which was advancing from Salamanca. Wilson retained half his force in Almeida and deployed the remainder in a screen of outposts beyond the Spanish fortress of Cuidad Rodrigo, some 20 miles into Spain. With commendable energy he repeatedly attacked and raided the French outposts and foraging parties. In doing so he convinced Lapisse that the French division was being confronted by a substantial allied force. Thus Lapisse, rather than marching into the Mondego Valley via Ciudad Rodrigo and Almeida as ordered, stood on the defensive at Salamanca. Wilson's and the Legion's action on the border played a significant part in the failure of the role to be played by Lapisse in the eastern arm of Napoleon's pincer movement on Northern Portugal; the more so that they were so heavily outnumbered.

The Lisbon Garrison

The strength of the garrison left at Lisbon was some 10,000 men, but this figure fluctuated with the arrival of reinforcements, departures to the army, attachments and detachments to Gibraltar, Cádiz and Sicily. The garrisons of Almeida and Elvas were reinstated with some of the battalions that had marched to join Sir John Moore that had turned back when Napoleon began his operations.

In the absence of an effective Portuguese army, the British garrison performed duties that included guards at the citadel and garrisoning the forts that covered the Tagus and the landward approaches to the city. For most, life in garrison was not difficult and those who had money were able to enjoy Lisbon, but already the army's twin afflictions of a lack of cash and arrears of pay were beginning to show.

In addition to the garrison battalions, there were the sick left in the depot hospital at Belém by the regiments that departed with Sir John Moore. A poor state of hygiene had led to typhoid in the camps outside Lisbon. Old campaigners would have been aware, even if they didn't know exactly why, that hygiene and camp cleanliness were important in order to avoid disease. Captain Leach of 2nd 95th was one of those who suffered and was confined to the hospital established at Belém. He wrote: 'Fevers and agues were extremely prevalent, and I was one of the many attacked, which confined me to my bed many weeks, and reduced me to a mere skeleton; so that it was more probable I should find my grave in Lisbon.'[8]

During January 1809, Brigadier Cameron organized and re-equipped the sick who had recovered, and those others left behind when Sir John Moore marched, into two battalions of detachments. This not only bolstered the garrison but organized men who, having regained their health, were becoming an increasing nuisance, into properly disciplined units. Over the following weeks further men were released from hospital and stragglers from the retreat to A Coruña were rounded up in the north of Portugal. A return made as early as 6 February gave the strength of the two battalions of detachments as 1,463 rank and file. Altogether these and some 3,000 stragglers from Sir John Moore's army boosted Cradock's strength.

The Future

With Sir John Moore killed at A Coruña and the army successfully evacuated back to England, it would not have been wrong to assume that for the British government, the Portuguese adventure was over, especially when one considers Moore's views regarding the defensibility of Portugal. During the autumn of 1808, based on little topographical knowledge of the country, he wrote to Lord Castlereagh:

> I can say generally that the frontier of Portugal is not defensible against a superior force. It is an open frontier, all equally rugged, but all equally to be penetrated. If the French succeed in Spain, it will be vain to attempt to resist them in Portugal.

When Castlereagh asked Wellesley about Sir John Moore's memorandum on the defence of Portugal, Sir Arthur replied on 9 March 1809, carefully gauging the situation and difficulties of the French, saying:

> I have always been of opinion that Portugal might be defended, whatever might be the result of the contest in Spain, and that in the meantime

measures adopted for the defence of Portugal would be highly useful to the Spaniards in their contest with the French. My notion was that the Portuguese military establishment ought to be revived, and that in addition to those troops His Majesty ought to employ about 20,000 British troops, including about 4,000 cavalry. My opinion was that, even if Spain should have been conquered, the French would not be able to overrun Portugal with a smaller force than 100,000 men. As long as the contest may continue in Spain, this force, if it could be placed in a state of activity, would be highly useful to the Spaniards, and might eventually decide the contest.[9]

The government was persuaded and, rather than withdrawing from the Peninsula or redeploying the force elsewhere, the decision was taken to return to Portugal. With Sir John Moore dead and Lieutenant General Wellesley absolved of involvement in the reprehensible Convention of Cintra, Sir Arthur, as the only available commander who had had significant success against the French on Continental Europe, was now the natural choice to lead this return. His success in 1808 placated those who thought his experience and achievements in India during the period 1797–1805 were not relevant to fighting the French.

Within a month Lieutenant General Sir Arthur Wellesley had been reappointed to command of the army in Portugal and reinforcements were on their way to confront a renewed French invasion of the country, with Marshal Soult having bloodily captured the city of Oporto.

A French general of division.

Lieutenant General Wellesley's orders for the 1808 Peninsular Expedition[1]

Sir,   Horse Guards, 14th June, 1808.

His Majesty having been graciously pleased to appoint you to the command of a detachment of his army, to be employed upon a particular service, I have to desire that you will be pleased to take the earliest opportunity to assume the commands of this force, and carry into effect such instructions as you may receive from his Majesty's Ministers.

The force, which his Majesty has been pleased to place under your command, consists of the following corps:

Royal Artillery	
Royal Staff Corps Detachment	
29th Foot	
*32nd do. 1st Battalion	With Major General Spencer
*50th do. do.	
*82nd do. do.	
*5th do. do.	
*9th do. do.	
*38th do. do.	
*40th do. do.	
60th do. 5th do.	To proceed from Cork
*71st do. 1st do.	
*91st do. do.	
95th four Companies	
4th Royal Vet. Battalion[2]	
[20th Light Dragoons]	

And the staff appointed to this force is composed as follows:-

Major General Spencer	Brig. General Nightingall
Major General Hill	Brig. General Fane
Major General Ferguson	Brig. General Caitlin Craufurd

On all subjects relating to your command, you will be pleased to correspond with me, and you will regularly communicate to me all military transactions, in which you may be engaged, reporting to me all vacancies that may occur in the troops under your command; and as the power of appointing to commissions is not vested in you, you will be pleased to recommend to me such officers as may appear to you most deserving of promotion, stating the special reasons, where such recommendations are not in the usual channel of seniority.

As the regiments marked thus (*), under your command, have second battalions attached to them, and which remain in this country, it is necessary that I should acquaint you, that the first battalions under your orders being composed exclusively of the senior officers of their respective ranks, such vacancies as may occur therein, by promotion or casualty, must unavoidably be supplied by officers from the second battalions, who will be ordered immediately to join, on such vacancies being made known to me.

Should you have occasion to recommend any gentleman for an ensigncy, you will be pleased to make known his address, in order that, if his Majesty should be pleased to confirm the recommendation, he may be directed to join the corps immediately on his appointment.

You will transmit, monthly, returns of the troops under your command, to the Secretary at War, and to the Adjutant General, for my information; and you will strictly adhere to his Majesty's regulations, in regard to the pay, clothing, and appointments of the troops; and your special attention must necessarily be directed to their discipline, and to the interior economy of the different corps, which is so essential, not only to the comfort of the soldier, but to the preservation of his health, under every change of climate to which he may be exposed.

Under the head of pay, I have to direct your attention to the instructions of the Paymasters General to their deputy, respecting the usual stoppages being deducted from the pay of the several Staff officers, and to which you are requested to give the most punctual attention.

You will be vested with the usual powers of convening General Courts Martial, upon which subject I have to observe that, as great inconvenience has arisen to the service from officers commanding on foreign stations having permitted prisoners to return to England prior to the proceedings and opinion of the Court Martial having been submitted to the King, I have to request that, in all cases, where any person whatever may be tried by a General Court Martial, and where your powers are not sufficient to enable you to decide finally upon the proceedings, opinion, and sentence of the Court, that you do not permit the prisoner to return to England until his Majesty's commands shall have been duly communicated to you through the proper channel for that purpose.

I have likewise to acquaint you, that as many General Officers, from the best motives, have taken upon themselves to commute sentences of capital punishment to transportation for a term of years, or for life, when it is found that no such power is delegated by his Majesty, and, consequently, that the whole of the proceedings may be thereby rendered nugatory, it will be necessary that your particular attention should be given to the powers granted to you by his Majesty's warrant on this subject, in order to prevent you from inadvertently falling into a similar irregularity.

It is particularly desirable that the officer, and the head of the Quarter Master General's staff, should be directed to keep a journal, or other memorandum, descriptive of the movements of the troops, and occurrences in which they are engaged; as also, that he should take and collect plans of the harbours, positions, or fortified places, in which the troops may be, for the purpose of being transmitted to me, and lodged in the military depôt.

In all points where any question or doubt may arise, and in which you may be desirous of receiving further and more specific instructions, you will always find me ready to pay the earliest attention to your representations.

I am, &c.
FREDERICK,
Commander in Chief

Lieut. Gen. Sir A. Wellesley, K.B.

*   *   *

It was more than two weeks later that Wellesley, by then back in Dublin, received his full orders from Lord Castlereagh, Secretary of State for War:

Downing Street, 30th June, 1808.

The occupation of Spain and Portugal by the troops of France, and the entire usurpation of their respective governments by that power, has determined his Majesty to direct a corps of his troops, as stated in the margin, to be prepared for service, to be employed, under your orders, in counteracting the designs of the enemy, and in affording to the Spanish and Portuguese nations every possible aid in throwing off the yoke of France.

You will receive, enclosed, the communications which have been made by the deputies of the principality of Asturias, and the kingdom of Galicia, to his Majesty's government, together with the reply which his Majesty has directed to be made to their demand of assistance.

I also enclose a statement of the supplies which have been already dispatched to the port of Gijon, for the use of the people of Asturias.

As the deputies from the above provinces do not desire the employment of any corps of his Majesty's troops in the quarter of Spain, from whence they are immediately delegated, but have rather pressed, as calculated to operate a powerful diversion in their power, the importance of directing the efforts of the British troops to the expulsion of the enemy from Portugal, that the insurrection against the French may thereby become general throughout that kingdom, as well as Spain, it is, therefore, deemed expedient that your attention should be immediately directed to that object.

The difficulty of returning to the northward, with a fleet of transports, at this season of the year, renders it expedient that you should, in the first instance, proceed with the armament under your orders off Cape Finisterre. You will, yourself, precede them in a fast sailing frigate to Coruña, where you will have the best means of learning the actual state of things, both in Spain and Portugal; and of judging how far the corps, under your immediate orders, either separately or reinforced by Major General Spencer's corps, can be considered as of sufficient strength to undertake an operation against the Tagus.

If you should be of opinion, from the information you may receive, that the enterprise in question cannot be undertaken without waiting for reinforcements from home, you will communicate, confidentially, to the Provisional Government of Galicia, that it is material to the interests of the common cause that your armament should be enabled to take an anchorage to the northward of the Tagus, till it can be supported by a further force from home; and you will make arrangements with them, for having permission to proceed with it to Vigo, where it is conceived it can remain with not less security than in the harbour of Ferrol, and from which it can proceed to the southward with more facility than from the latter port.

In case you should go into Vigo, you will send orders to Major General Spencer to join you at that place, should he have arrived off the Tagus, in consequence of the enclosed orders; and you will also transmit home such information as may enable his Majesty's ministers to take measures for supporting your corps from hence.

With a view to the contingency of your force being deemed unequal to the operation, an additional corps of 10,000 men has been ordered to be prepared for service, and which, it is hoped, may be ready to proceed in about three weeks from the present time. I enclose such information as we are in possession of with respect to the enemy's force in Portugal; a considerable proportion of which is said to have been lately moved to Almeida, on the north- eastern frontier. You will, no doubt, be enabled to obtain more recent information at Coruña, in aid of which

Lieut. Colonel Browne has been ordered to proceed to Oporto, and to meet you, with such intelligence as he can procure, off Cape Finisterre.

An officer of engineers, acquainted with the defences of the Tagus, has also been sent off the Tagus to make observations, and to prepare information for your consideration with respect to the execution of the proposed attack on the Tagus. The result of his inquiries he will be directed to transmit also to the rendezvous off Cape Finisterre, remaining himself off the Tagus till your arrival.

You are authorised to give the most distinct assurances to the Spanish and Portuguese people, that his Majesty, in sending a force to their assistance, has no other object in view than to afford them the most unqualified and disinterested support; and in any arrangements that you may be called upon to make with either nation, in the prosecution of the common cause, you will act with the utmost liberality and confidence, and upon the principle that his Majesty's endeavours are to be directed to aid the people of Spain and Portugal in restoring and maintaining against France the independence and integrity of their respective monarchies. In the rapid succession in which events must be expected to follow each other, situated as Spain and Portugal now are, much must be left to your judgement and decision on the spot. His Majesty is graciously pleased to confide to you the fullest discretion to act according to circumstances, for the benefit of his service, and you may rely on your measures being favourably interpreted, and receiving the most cordial support.

You will facilitate, as much as possible, communications between the respective provinces and colonies of Spain, and reconcile, by your good offices, any differences that may arise between them in the execution of the common purpose. Should any serious division of sentiment occur, with respect to the nature of the Provisional Government which is to act during the present interregnum, or with respect to the Prince in whose name the legal authority is considered as vested by the captivity or abdication of certain branches of the royal family, you will avoid, as far as possible, taking any part in such discussions, without the express authority of your government.

You will, however, impress upon the minds of persons in authority, that, consistently with the effectual assertion of their independence, they cannot possibly acknowledge the King or Prince of Asturias, as, at present, possessing any authority whatever, or consider any act done by them as valid, until they return within the country, and become absolutely free agents. That they never can be considered free so long as they shall be prevailed on to acquiesce in the continuance of French troops either in Spain or Portugal.

The entire and absolute evacuation of the Peninsula, by the troops of France, being, after what has lately passed, the only security for Spanish independence, and the only basis upon which the Spanish nation should be prevailed upon to treat or to lay down their arms.

I have the honour to be, &c.
CASTLEREAGH.

A French infantryman serving with a line regiment's centre company.

Appendix II

Lieutenant General Wellesley's Roliça Dispatch

My Lord,   Villa Verde, 17th Aug. 1808.
The French General Laborde [*sic*] having continued in his position at Roliça, since my arrival at Caldas on the 15th instant, I determined to attack him in it this morning. Roliça is situated on an eminence, having a plain in its front, at the end of a valley, which commences at Caldas, and is closed to the south-ward by mountains, which join the hills forming the valley on the left. Looking from Caldas, in the centre of the valley, and about 8 miles from Roliça is the town and old Moorish fort of Óbidos, from whence the enemy's picquets had been driven on the 15th; and from that time he had posts in the hills on both sides of the valley, as well as in the plain in front of his army, which was posted on the heights in front of Roliça, its right resting upon the hills, its left upon an eminence on which was a windmill, and the whole covering four or five passes into the mountains on his rear.

I have reason to believe that his force consisted of at least 6,000 men, of which about 500 were cavalry, with five pieces of cannon; and there was some reason to believe that General Loison, who was at Rio Mayor yesterday, would join General Laborde by his right in the course of the night.

The plan of attack was formed accordingly, and the army having broken up from Caldas this morning, was formed into three columns. The right, con-sisting of 1,200 Portuguese infantry, 50 Portuguese cavalry, destined to turn the enemy's left, and penetrate into the mountains in his rear. The left, con-sisting of Major General Ferguson's and Brigadier General Bowes's brigade of infantry, three companies of riflemen, a brigade of light artillery, and twenty British and twenty Portuguese cavalry, was destined, under the com-mand of Major General Ferguson, to ascend the hills at Óbidos, to turn all the enemy's posts on the left of the valley, as well as the right of his post at Roliça. This corps was also destined to watch the motions of General Loison on the enemy's right, who I had heard had moved from Rio Mayor towards Alcoentre last night. The centre column, consisting of Major General Hill's, Brigadier General Nightingall's, Brigadier General Craufurd's, and Brigadier General Fane's brigades (with the exception of the riflemen detached with Major General Ferguson), and 400 Portuguese light infantry, the British and

167

Portuguese cavalry, a brigade of 9-pounders, and a brigade of 6-pounders, was destined to attack General Laborde's position in the front.

The columns being formed, the troops moved from Óbidos about seven o'clock in the morning. Brigadier General Fane's riflemen were immediately detached into the hills on the left of the valley, to keep up the communication between the centre and left columns, and to protect the march of the former along the valley, and the enemy's posts were successively driven in. Major General Hill's brigade, formed in three columns of battalions, moved on the right of the valley, supported by the cavalry, in order to attack the enemy's left; and Brigadier Generals Nightingall and Craufurd moved with the artillery along the high road, until at length the former formed in the plain immediately in the enemy's front, supported by the light infantry companies, and the 45th regiment of Brigadier General Craufurd's brigade; while the two other regiments of this brigade (the 50th and 91st) and half of the 9-pounder brigade were kept as a reserve in the rear.

Major General Hill and Brigadier General Nightingall advanced upon the enemy's position, and at the same moment Brigadier General Fane's riflemen were in the hills on his right, the Portuguese in a village upon his left, and Major General Ferguson's column was descending from the heights into the plain. From this situation the enemy retired by the passes into the mountains with the utmost regularity and the greatest celerity; and notwithstanding the rapid advance of the British infantry, the want of a sufficient body of cavalry was the cause of his suffering but little loss on the plain.

It was then necessary to make a disposition to attack the formidable position which he had taken up.

Brigadier General Fane's riflemen were already in the mountains on his right, and no time was lost in attacking the different passes, as well to support the riflemen as to defeat the enemy completely.

The Portuguese infantry were ordered to move up a pass on the right of the whole. The light companies of Major General Hill's brigade, and the 5th regiment, moved up a pass next on the right; and the 29th regiment, supported by the 9th regiment under Brigadier General Nightingall, a third pass; and the 45th and 82nd regiments passes on the left.

These passes were all difficult of access, and some of them were well defended by the enemy, particularly that which was attacked by the 29th and 9th regiments. These regiments attacked with the utmost impetuosity, and reached the enemy before those whose attacks were to be made on their flanks.

The defence of the enemy was desperate, and it was in this attack principally that we sustained the loss which we have to lament, particularly of that gallant officer, the Honourable Lieut. Colonel Lake, who distinguished himself upon this occasion. The enemy was, however, driven from all the positions he had taken in the passes of the mountains, and our troops were advanced in the plains on their tops. For a considerable length of time the 29th and 9th regiments alone were advanced to this point, with Brigadier General Fane's riflemen at a distance on the left, and they were afterwards supported by the 5th regiment, and by the light companies of Major General Hill's brigade, which had come upon their right, and by the other troops ordered to ascend the mountains, who came up by degrees.

The enemy here made three most gallant attacks upon the 29th and 9th regiments, supported as I have above stated, with a view to cover the retreat of his defeated army, in all of which he was, however, repulsed; but he succeeded in effecting his retreat in good order, owing principally to my want of cavalry; and secondly, to the difficulty of bringing up the passes of the mountains with celerity a sufficient number of troops and of cannon to support those which had first ascended. The loss of the enemy has, however, been very great, and he left three pieces of cannon in our hands.

I cannot sufficiently applaud the conduct of the troops throughout this action. The enemy's positions were formidable, and he took them up with his usual ability and celerity and defended them most gallantly. But I must observe, that although we had such a superiority of numbers employed in the operations of this day, the troops actually engaged in the heat of the action were, from unavoidable circumstances, only the 5th, 9th, 29th, the riflemen of the 95th and 60th, and the flank companies of Major General Hill's brigade; being a number by no means equal to that of the enemy. Their conduct therefore deserves the highest commendations.

I cannot avoid taking this opportunity of expressing my acknowledgements for the aid and support I received from all the General and other officers of this army: I am particularly indebted to Major General Spencer for the advice and assistance I received from him; to Major General Ferguson, for the manner in which he led the left column; and to Major General Hill, and Brigadier Generals Nightingall and Fane, for the manner in which they conducted the different attacks which they led.

I derived most material assistance also from Lieut. Colonel Tucker and Lieut. Colonel Bathurst, in the offices of Deputy Adjutant and Deputy Quarter Master General, and from the officers of the staff employed under them. I must also mention that I had every reason to be satisfied with the artillery under Lieut. Colonel Robe. I have the honour to enclose herewith a return of killed, wounded, and missing.

I have the honour to be, &c.
ARTHUR WELLESLEY

Viscount Castlereagh

Essential tools used for the maintenance of musket and rifle

Tin of brick dust and oil
for cleaning off rust.

Musket tool on a leather
thong,; used for changing
flints and running repairs.

Worm for removing a
cartridge from a barrel.

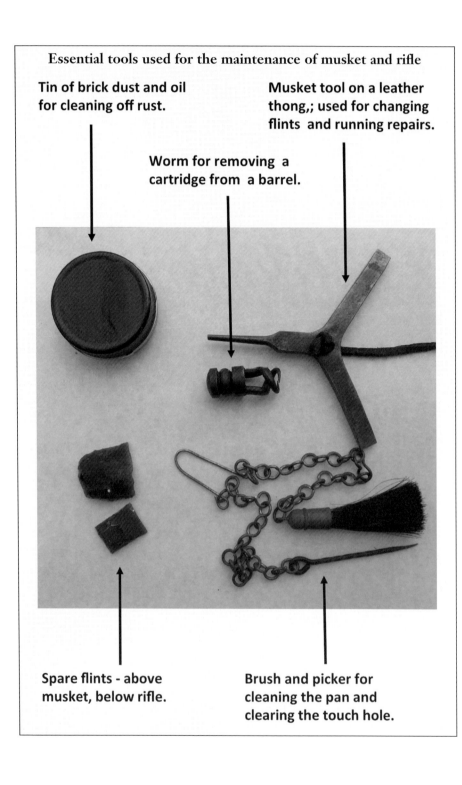

Spare flints - above
musket, below rifle.

Brush and picker for
cleaning the pan and
clearing the touch hole.

Lieutenant General Wellesley's Campaign Plan

With the army ashore and preparing to march south on Lisbon, Wellesley outlined his campaign plan to Admiral Cotton and his part in it.

To Admiral Sir Charles Cotton   Lavos, 8th Aug. 1808.

I have the honour to enclose the copy of a letter which I have written to Captain Malcolm of H.M.S. *Donegal*, which contains the result of a conference which I have had with him upon the subject of the disposal of the fleet of transports; of which I hope that you will approve.

I would suggest that Captain Malcolm should remain here till the army will be well advanced towards Lisbon, and that then he should go down the coast with the fleet.

The ships which will go under convoy of the *Alfred* contain all that can be wanted either to supply the army with provisions or ammunition; or with equipments for the attack of Peniche, if upon my arrival in that quarter I should find it expedient to undertake it.

I propose to march on Wednesday with my own corps and General Spencer's, consisting of about 10,000 men and about 5,000 Portuguese troops, towards Lisbon; which place I shall approach by Mafra, and thence by the heights to the northward of the city.

You will observe that the Veteran Battalion is ordered to join your fleet off the Tagus. This corps, which consists of [blank in manuscript] men, is eventually destined for the garrison of Gibraltar; it is a good corps, but the soldiers being old, and disabled by wounds and otherwise for active service, cannot march. I have therefore sent them to the fleet off the Tagus, in order that the enemy may be induced to believe that we intend to make an attack in that quarter; and I beg leave to suggest that when the army will approach the neighbourhood of Mafra and Cintra, of which I shall be able to give you intelligence by the aid of Captain Malcolm or of Captain Bligh, you should make an attack with this corps and the marines upon the Bay of Guinsha or such other in the neighbourhood of the Rock of Lisbon as you may think most likely to be successful, and to afford a diversion in our favour.

Admiral Sir Charles Cotton commanded a Royal Naval squadron blockading the west coast of Iberia, especially the blockading of a Russian squadron in the Tagus at Lisbon.

Besides the corps already landed which will move forward on the day after to-morrow under my command, I expect 5,000 men from England under the command of Brigadier-General Acland; and in a short time 10,000 men under the command of Lieutenant-General Sir Harry Burrard.

I propose to leave orders for the first to proceed along the coast from hence, and to communicate with Captain Bligh of the *Alfred*, through whose means I intend to give them their ulterior orders. My present intention is to employ this corps in the attack of Peniche, if it should be necessary to have possession of that place at an early period, and it should be impossible to obtain it excepting by a regular attack. If I should not find the possession of Peniche to be necessary, I propose to order this corps to join the fleet off the Tagus; and I recommend that they should be landed as I have above suggested that the Veteran Battalion and the marines should, when the army under my command will approach sufficiently near to render it impossible for the enemy to throw his whole force upon them.

In case the 10,000 men under Sir Harry Burrard should arrive during the continuance of my operations upon Lisbon, I intend to leave a letter to suggest to Sir Harry that they should be landed here, and march from hence towards Santarém upon the Tagus.

The object of this movement will be that they will be in a situation to cut off the enemy's retreat, whether he will attempt to make it by Almeida or by Elvas; at the same time that they will protect the rear of the army under my command, in case the enemy should detach any force from Spain into Portugal.

I shall be obliged to you if you will favour me with your sentiments upon the plan of operations above suggested.

I have, &c.,
ARTHUR WELLESLEY.

The Pelisse

The pelisse, originating from Hungarian hussars during the seventeenth century, was originally a short fur-trimmed and braided jacket often worn hanging loose over the left shoulder, ostensibly to provide some protection from sword cuts. During the eighteenth century the fashionable wearing of the pelisse by light cavalry swept west across Europe. In Britain from 1800, although 'Hungarianisation' was stoutly resisted by George III, the pelisse gained increasing popularity and was adopted by some light dragoon regiments, usually those with influential royal colonels, namely the Duke of York and the Prince of Wales.* By 1808 adoption of the hussar-style uniform was a fait accompli and the King issued the Hussar Warrant for a strictly limited number of light cavalry regiments to be styled 'Light Dragoons (Hussars)'. This effectively regulated fashion.

Even though clearly of little used in the Iberian summer, the Hungarian pelisse style was more than a fashion statement on campaign. It was a practical over jacket with those designed to be worn during winter and inclement weather, rather than for parade, being made of heavier overcoating weight wool cloth.

Wearing of the pelisse was not confined to the cavalry nor as a short jacket. In 1801, when the Rifle Corps was formally established, the officers' uniform in particular was styled on the light cavalry, with the aim being to place the regiment alongside that glamorous arm. Not only was this designed to recruit 'the right sort

* Townsend, Ben, *Fashioning Regulation and Regulating Fashion: The Uniforms of the British Army 1800–1815*, Vol. 1 (Helion & Co, Solihull, 2018).

An officer of the 95th Rifles wearing a pelisse. The trimming for field officers was dark fur and for more junior officers, wool.

of chaps' but along with the green uniform, it was a deliberate measure to set them apart from the infantry of the line. The only other infantry regiment known to have adopted the pelisse for their officers was the 43rd Light Infantry, also from the Light Brigade/Division. In their case the colour of the material was probably grey.

A Brunswick Hussar officer wearing his pelisse. Note the luxurious lining.

The uniform of the Royal Horse Artillery was also styled on the light cavalry and the officers had adopted the pelisse by 1805, with black lacing trimmed with dark fur.

During the winter of 1809/10 Viscount Wellington is recorded as wearing a long pelisse jacket or coat. This may indicate it may have been worn more widely on campaign, probably by fashionable staff and commanders.

The pelisse style was one of those copied into ladies' fashion, in this case based on the 95th Rifles.

Lieutenant General Wellesley's Vimeiro Dispatch

Sir Arthur's dispatch was addressed to Lieutenant General Sir Harry Burrard who, by the time the dispatch was completed on the evening of the 21 August, had landed and taken command of the army. It was copied and forwarded to Horseguards.

Sir,   Vimeiro, 21st August 1808.

I have the honour to inform you, that the enemy attacked us in our position at Vimeiro this morning.

The village of Vimeiro stands in a valley, through which runs the River Maceira; at the back, and to the westward and northward of this village, is a mountain, the western point of which touches the sea, and the eastern is separated by a deep ravine from the heights, over which passes the road which leads from Lourinha, and then northward to Vimeiro. The greater part of the infantry, the 1st, 2nd, 3rd, 4th, 5th, and 8th brigades were posted on this mountain, with eight pieces of artillery, Major General Hill's brigade being on the right, and Major General Ferguson's on the left, having one battalion on the heights separated from the mountain. On the eastern and southern side of the town is a mill, which is entirely commanded, particularly on its right, by the mountain to the westward of the town, and commanding all the ground in the neighbourhood to the southward and eastward, on which Brigadier General Fane was posted with his riflemen, and the 50th regiment, and Brigadier General Anstruther with his brigade, with half a brigade of 6-pounders, and half a brigade of 9-pounders, which had been ordered to the position in the course of last night. The ground over which passes the road from Lourinha commanded the left of this height, and it had not been occupied, excepting by a picquet [*sic*], as the camp had been taken up only for one night, and there was no water in the neighbourhood of this height.

The cavalry and the reserve of artillery were in the valley, between the hills on which the infantry stood, both flanking and supporting Brigadier General Fane's advanced guard.

The enemy first appeared about eight o'clock in the morning, in large bodies of cavalry on our left, upon the heights on the road to Lourinha;

and it was soon obvious, that the attack would be made upon our advanced guard and the left of our position; and Major General Ferguson's brigade was immediately moved across the ravine to the heights on the road to Lourinha, with three pieces of cannon; he was followed successively by Brigadier General Nightingall, with his brigade and three pieces of cannon; Brigadier General Acland, and his brigade; and Brigadier General Bowes, with his brigade. These troops were formed (Major General Ferguson's brigade in the first line, Brigadier General Nightingall's in the second, and Brigadier General Bowes's and Acland's in columns in the rear) on those heights with their right upon the valley which leads into Vimeiro; and their left upon the other ravine, which separates these heights from the range which terminates at the landing place at Maceira. On the last mentioned heights, the Portuguese troops, which had been in the bottom near Vimeiro, were posted in the first instance, and they were supported by Brigadier General Craufurd's brigade.

The troops of the advanced guard, on the heights to the southward and eastward of the town, were deemed sufficient for its defence, and Major General Hill was moved to the centre of the mountain, on which the great body of the infantry had been posted, as a support to these troops, and as a reserve to the whole army; in addition to this support, these troops had that of the cavalry in the rear of their right.

The enemy's attack began in several columns upon the whole of the troops on this height; on the left they advanced, notwithstanding the fire of the riflemen, close to the 50th regiment, and they were checked and driven back only by the bayonets of that corps. The 2nd battalion 43rd regiment was likewise closely engaged with them, in the road which leads into Vimeiro; a part of that corps having been ordered into the churchyard, to prevent them from penetrating into the town. On the right of the position they were repulsed by the bayonets of the 97th regiment, whose corps was successfully supported by the 2nd battalion 52nd, which, by an advance in column, took the enemy in flank.

Besides this opposition given to the attack of the enemy on the advanced guard by their own exertions, they were attacked in flank by Brigadier General Acland's brigade, in its advance to its position on the heights on the left, and a cannonade was kept up on the flank of the enemy's columns by the artillery on those heights.

At length, after a most desperate contest, the enemy was driven back in confusion from this attack, with the loss of seven pieces of cannon, many prisoners, and a great number of officers and soldiers killed and wounded. He was pursued by a detachment of the 20th light dragoons, but the enemy's cavalry were so much superior in numbers, that this detachment has suffered much, and Lieut. Colonel Taylor was unfortunately killed.

Nearly at the same time the enemy's attack commenced upon the heights on the road to Lourinha; this attack was supported by a large body of cavalry, and was made with the usual impetuosity of French troops. It was received with steadiness by Major General Ferguson's brigade, consisting of the 36th, 40th, and 71st regiments, and these corps charged as soon as the enemy approached them, who gave way, and they continued to advance upon him, supported by the 82nd, one of the corps of Brigadier General Nightingall's brigade, which, as the ground extended, afterwards formed a part of the first line by the 29th regiment, and by Brigadier General Bowes's and Acland's brigades: whilst Brigadier General Craufurd's brigade and the Portuguese troops, in two lines, advanced along the height on the left. In the advance of Major General Ferguson's brigade, six pieces of cannon were taken from the enemy, with many prisoners, and vast numbers were killed and wounded.

The enemy afterwards made an attempt to recover part of his artillery, by attacking the 71st and 82nd regiments, which were halted in a valley in which it had *been* taken. These regiments retired from the low grounds in the valley to the heights, where they halted, faced about and fired, and advanced upon the enemy, who had by that time arrived in the low ground, and they thus obliged him again to retire with great loss.

In this action, in which the whole of the French force in Portugal was employed, under the command of the Duke D'Abrantes in person, in which the enemy was certainly superior in cavalry and artillery, and in which not more than half of the British army was actually engaged, he has sustained a signal defeat, and has lost thirteen pieces of cannon, twenty-three ammunition waggons, with powder, shells, stores of all descriptions, and 20,000 rounds of musket ammunition. One General officer has been wounded (Brenier) and taken prisoner, and a great many officers and soldiers have been killed, wounded, and taken.

The valour and discipline of his Majesty's troops have been conspicuous upon this occasion, as you, who witnessed the greatest part of the action, must have observed; but it is a justice to the following corps to draw your notice to them in a particular manner: viz., the Royal artillery, commanded by Lieut. Colonel Robe; the 20th light dragoons, which has been commanded by Lieut. Colonel Taylor: the 50th regiment, commanded by Colonel Walker; the 2nd battalion 95th foot, commanded by Major Travers; the 5th battalion 60th regiment, commanded by Major Davy; the 2nd battalion 43rd, commanded by Major Hull; the 2nd battalion 52nd, commanded by Lieut. Colonel Ross; the 97th regiment, commanded by Lieut. Colonel Lyon; the 36th regiment, commanded by Colonel Burne; the 40th, commanded by Lieut. Colonel Kemmis; the 71st, commanded by Lieut. Colonel Pack; and the 82nd regiment, commanded by Major Eyre.

In mentioning Colonel Burne and the 36th regiment upon this occasion, I cannot avoid adding that the regular and orderly conduct of this corps throughout the service, and their gallantry and discipline in action, have been conspicuous.

I must take this opportunity of acknowledging my obligations to the General and Staff Officers of the army. I was much indebted to Major General Spencer's judgement and experience in the decision which I formed in respect to the number of troops allotted to each point of defence, *and* for his advice and assistance throughout the action. In the position taken up by Major General Ferguson's brigade, and in its advances upon the enemy, that officer showed equal bravery and judgement, and much praise is due to Brigadier General Fane and Brigadier General Anstruther for their gallant defence of their position in front of Vimeiro, and to Brigadier General Nightingall for the manner in which he supported the attack upon the enemy made by Major General Ferguson.

Lieut. Colonel G. Tucker, and Lieut. Colonel Bathurst, and the officers in the departments of the Adjutant and Quartermaster General, and Lieut. Colonel Torrent and the officers of my personal staff, rendered me the greatest assistance throughout the action.

I have the honour to enclose herewith a return of the killed, wounded, and missing.

I have the honour to be, &c.

Lieut. Gen. Sir Harry Burrard.   ARTHUR WELLESLEY.

P.S. Since writing the above I have been informed that a French General officer, supposed to be General Thiebault the chief of the Staff, has been found dead upon the field of battle.

A. W.

The Convention of Cintra[1]

The convention in general terms agreed by Dalrymple, Burrard and Wellesley was negotiated in detail by Lieutenant Colonel Murray and General Kellermann, was not well received at home and widely seen then as now as being unduly lenient towards the French, with Article XV being a prime example.

ENCLOSURE DRAFT OF THE DEFINITIVE CONVENTION
FOR THE EVACUATION OF PORTUGAL BY THE
FRENCH ARMY

The Generals Commanding in Chief the British and French armies in Portugal having determined to negotiate and conclude a treaty for the evacuation of Portugal by the French troops on the basis of the agreement entered into on the 22nd instant for a suspension of hostilities have appointed the undermentioned officers to negotiate the same in their names. Viz, on the part of the General in Chief of the British army Lieutenant Colonel Murray Quartermaster General and on the part of the General in Chief of the French army Monsieur Kellermann General of Division to whom they have given authority to negotiate and conclude a Convention to that effect subject to their ratification respectively and to that of the Admiral commanding the British fleet at the entrance of the Tagus. These two officers after exchanging their full powers have agreed upon the articles which follow:

ARTICLE I
All the places and forts in the kingdom of Portugal occupied by the French troops shall be delivered up to the British army in the state in which they are at the period of the signature of the present Convention.

ARTICLE II
The French troops shall evacuate Portugal with their arms and baggage, they shall not be considered as prisoners of war, and on their arrival in France they shall be at liberty to serve.

ARTICLE III
The English government shall furnish at its expense the means of conveyance for the French army which shall be disembarked in any of the ports of France between Rochefort and Lorient inclusively.

ARTICLE IV

The French army shall carry with it all its artillery of French calibre with the horses belonging to it and the tumbrils supplied with sixty rounds per gun.

ARTICLE V

The French army shall carry with it all its equipments and all that is comprehended under the name of property of the army; that is to say its military chest and the carriages attached to the field commissariat and field hospitals or shall be allowed to dispose of such part of the same on its account as the Commander in Chief may judge it unnecessary to embark. In like manner all individuals of the army shall be at liberty to dispose of their private property of every description with full security hereafter for the purchasers.

ARTICLE VI

The cavalry are to embark their horses and the Generals and other officers the number of horses allowed to each by the regulations of the French service. It is however fully understood that the means of conveyance for horses at the disposal of the British Commanders are very limited. Some additional conveyance may be procured in the port of Lisbon and at all events every facility will be given to the French army to dispose of the horses belonging to it which cannot be embarked.

ARTICLE VII

In order to facilitate the embarkation, it shall take place in three divisions, the last of which will be principally composed of the garrisons of the places of the cavalry, the artillery, the sick and the equipments of the army.

ARTICLE VIII

The garrison of Elvas and its forts and of Peniche and Palmella will be embarked at Lisbon, that of Almeida at Oporto, or the nearest harbour. They will be accompanied on their march by British Commissaries charged with providing for their subsistence and accommodation.

ARTICLE IX

All the sick and wounded who cannot be embarked with the troops are entrusted to the British army. They are to be taken care of whilst they remain in this country at the expense of the British government under the condition of the same being reimbursed by France when the final evacuation is effected. The English government will provide for their return to France which shall take place by detachments of about 150 or 200 men at a time. A sufficient number of French medical officers shall be left behind to attend them.

ARTICLE X

As soon as the vessels employed to convey the army to France shall have disembarked it in the harbours specified or in any others of the ports of France to which stress of weather may force them, every facility shall be given them to return to England without delay and security against capture until their arrival in a friendly port.

ARTICLE XI

The French army shall be concentrated in Lisbon and within a distance of about two leagues from it. The English army will approach within three leagues of the capital and will be so placed as to leave about one league between the two armies.

ARTICLE XII

The fortresses of Elvas, Peniche, Almeida and Palmella shall be given up as soon as the British troops can arrive to occupy them. In the meantime, the General in Chief of the British army will give notice of the present Convention to the garrisons of those places as also to the troops before them in order to put a stop to all further hostilities. The occupation of Lisbon and of the forts of St Julian and the Bugio together with the other defences of the Tagus shall take place on the embarkation of the second division of the French army. Immediately on the exchange of the ratifications the British troops shall be put in possession of the forts of Cascaes and the other forts to the right of St Julian's.

ARTICLE XIII

The transports destined for the embarkation and such ships of war as may be necessary towards that service shall be immediately admitted into the Tagus not exceeding three.

ARTICLE XIV

Commissaries shall be named on both sides to regulate and accelerate the execution of the arrangements agreed upon.

ARTICLE XV

Should there arise doubts as to the meaning of any Article it will be explained favourably to the French army.

ARTICLE XVI

From the date of the ratification of the present Convention by the Commanders in Chief by land and sea all contributions or requisitions shall cease throughout Portugal on the part of the French army.

ARTICLE XVII

All subjects of France or of powers in friendship or alliance with France domiciliated in Portugal or accidentally in this country shall be protected, their property of every kind moveable and immoveable shall be respected and they shall be at liberty either to accompany the French army or to remain in Portugal. In either case their property is guaranteed to them with the liberty of retaining or of disposing of it and passing the produce of the sale thereof into France or any other country where they may fix their residence, the space of one year being allowed them for that purpose.

ARTICLE XVIII

No native of Portugal shall be rendered accountable for his political conduct during the period of the occupation of this country by the French army and all those who have continued in the exercise of their employments or who have accepted situations under the French government are placed under the protection of the British Commanders. They shall sustain no injury in their persons or property it not having been at their option to be obedient or not to the French government. They are also at liberty to avail themselves of the stipulations of the seventeenth Article.

ARTICLE XIX

The Spanish prisoners detained on board ship in the port of Lisbon shall be given up to the General in Chief of the British army who engages to obtain permission of the Spaniards to restore such French subjects either military or civil as may have been detained in Spain without being taken in battle or in consequence of military operations but on occasion of the occurrences of the 28th of last May and the days immediately following.

ARTICLE XX

There shall be an immediate exchange established for all ranks of prisoners made in Portugal since the commencement of the present hostilities.

ARTICLE XXI

Hostages shall be mutually given for the guarantee of the present Convention until its final completion.

ARTICLE XXII

It shall be allowed to the General in Chief of the French army to send an officer to France with intelligence of the present Convention. A vessel will be furnished by the British Admiral to convey him to Bordeaux or Rochefort.

ARTICLE XXIII

The British Admiral will be invited to accommodate his Excellency the Commander in Chief and the other principal officers of the French army on board ships of war.

Done and concluded at Lisbon this twenty-eighth day of August one thousand eight hundred and eight.

Appendix VI

On the March

For many of the soldiers in the heat of the 1808 Iberian summer, the marches of Wellesley's army south from Lavos or Maceira Bay were sore trials even for those that arrived after Vimeiro, as explained by Lieutenant Blakeney of the 28th Foot:

> This, our first march, although but of three leagues, was severely felt ... we had been for upward of four months cooped up in miserable little transports. The men had scarcely the use of their limbs; and being so long unaccustomed to carry their packs, to which were now added three days' provisions and sixty rounds of ball-cartridge, in this their first march, with the thermometer between ninety and a hundred, many were left behind and slowly followed after. The 4th or King's Own Regiment, with whom we were then brigaded, from its seniority of number, marched in front. Although at the time perhaps the finest looking body of men in the Army, the select of three battalions, yet, being generally rather advanced in age as soldiers and heavy-bodied, they were on this day continually falling out of the ranks and flanking the road. This afforded an opportunity to one of our light hardy Irishmen ... to remark: 'Faith! This is a very deceiving march; the royal milestones are so close to each other.'[1]

Not only did men fall out of the ranks, but some died of heat exhaustion. Rifleman Harris provides an insight into the reasons why:

> Being immediately pushed forwards up the country in advance of the main body, many of us, in this hot climate, very soon began to find out the misery of the frightful load we were condemned to march and fight under, with a burning sun above our heads, and our feet sinking every step into the hot sand.
>
> The weight I myself toiled under was tremendous, and I often wonder at the strength I possessed at this period, which enabled me to endure it; for, indeed, I am convinced that many of our infantry sank and died under the weight of their knapsacks alone. For my own part, being a handicraft, I marched under a weight sufficient to impede the free motions of a donkey; for besides my well-filled kit, there was the great-coat rolled on its top, my blanket and camp kettle, my haversack, stuffed full of leather

185

for repairing the men's shoes, together with a hammer and other tools (the lapstone I took the liberty of flinging to the devil), ship-biscuit and beef for three days. I also carried my canteen filled with water, my hatchet and rifle, and eighty rounds of ball cartridge in my pouch.

Altogether the quantity of things I had on my shoulders was enough and more than enough for my wants, sufficient, indeed, to sink a little fellow of 5 feet 7 inches into the earth. Nay, so awkwardly was the load our men bore in those days, placed upon their backs, that the free motion of the body was impeded, the head held down from the pile at the back of the neck, and the soldier half beaten before he came to the scratch.

Captain Patterson of the 50th Foot almost certainly refers to the more relaxed marches after Vimeiro. Clearly with the passage of years, he seems to have forgotten that as a captain he was mounted, and also the pain and sundry

The soldier's knapsack and greatcoat. Full Marching Order. There is evidence that the Rifles and light battalions were issued with the lightweight camp kettle pictured here long before the rest of the army in 1813.

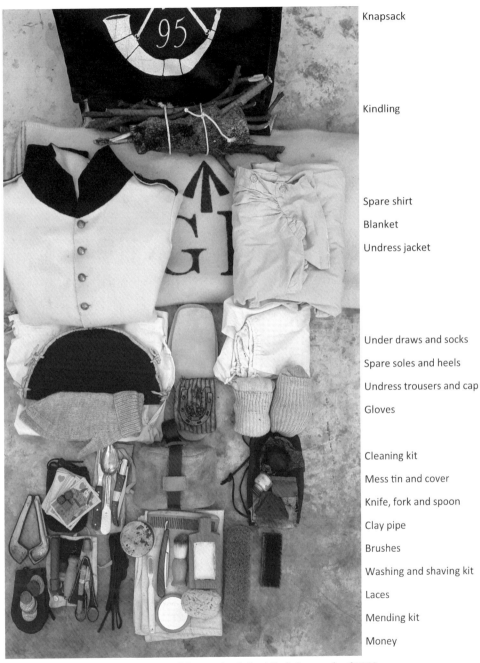

Knapsack

Kindling

Spare shirt

Blanket

Undress jacket

Under draws and socks

Spare soles and heels

Undress trousers and cap

Gloves

Cleaning kit

Mess tin and cover

Knife, fork and spoon

Clay pipe

Brushes

Washing and shaving kit

Laces

Mending kit

Money

The typical contents of the overloaded soldier's knapsack of 1808.

difficulties of a march as recalled by many, and he paints a rosy but none-theless informative picture of a typical route in 1808:[2]

> Once fairly on the road, it is astonishing how rapidly the hours glide away. The formalities of parade or drill marching are now at an end, and everyone indulges in that mode of perambulation which best suits him [marching at ease]. When the commanding officer is not one of your strict disciplinarians, the regimental juniors congregate together in groups, some in front, some in rear; while the men, though keeping their sections, travel in open ranks, filling the entire space of ground over which the route extends.
>
> At the head of the column is to be seen a host of seniors, or old hands, among whom the laugh and joke prevail; and there many a long-winded veteran inflicts upon the ears of his patient auditors a narrative as endless as the road. Ever and anon the second Major falls back, and, in order to shew his consequence and zeal, especially if a General with his staff should chance to be passing, he calls out, in a most important tone, 'Gentlemen, get into your places!' 'Keep on the flanks!' and other friendly admonitions. As soon as he is convinced, by the approving looks of the great man with the long feather and epaulettes, that his vigilance has been duly noticed, he gallops off to his old station, and the gentlemen betake themselves again to theirs, till another appearance of the chief, when the stray sheep are again called back to the flock. By the by, I know of nothing else that these second Majors have to do, unless it be to act the part of moveable pivots for dressing up the line (in which they are generally very fussy), or in whipping-in the young subalterns, whom they endeavour to keep in order.
>
> The surgeon, who is often a very hearty fellow, with better things than boluses and pill boxes in his panniers – together with the adjutant, and his brethren of the staff, attract around them, in the rear, a batch of thoroughly pleasant men, who keep up such a volley of jest and drollery, as frequently to beguile the weariness of the longest march. Thanks to their amusing powers, we have often found ourselves at the gates of the town, or on the campground, without being aware that we had travelled any distance.
>
> At intervals of one or two hours, each day, the troops are halted for a few minutes' rest. Then, all, as if by magic wand, are quickly squatted, and haversack being called for, the whole of them, like hungry cormorants at their prey, are soon engaged in one grand scene of mastication. Some perform a solo on the shank-bone of a well-picked ham; others display their talents on the drumstick of a half-starved fowl, while the majority gnaw their way through the skinny hunk of a tough old bullock. The

A miniature of an unknown officer of the 50th Foot, believed to have been painted in Dublin. He is wearing silver flank company wings with black facings. The regiment's nickname was 'The Dirty Half-Hundred'.

vultures and other birds of evil omen are, meanwhile, hovering in mid-air, ready to pounce upon the remnants of the feast when we are gone.

At the well-known sound of pipes, or bugle, the warriors are again (to use a parliamentary phrase) on their legs, stretching them out with renewed vigour. Among the soldiers there is likewise much of drollery and mirth, nothing makes much difference with them – it matters not whether trumps turn up or not; whether the chance be a battle, or a good billet, they are still the same, and trudge along devoid of care. Give them their allowance, and a little rest, and they require no more. Day after day I have listened to their jokes and stories and been highly entertained by their originality and humour.

Relatively straightforward marches may have been the routine, but the ones most oft remembered and described by diarists are those where the commissariat had failed, where there was particularly bad weather or a retreat in the presence of the enemy. These circumstances were ubiquitously terrible for the army.

French light infantrymen of the 9th *Légère*, the regiment Napoleon nicknamed 'The Incomparable'.

French and British Order of Battle at Vimeiro

British Army
(Lieutenant General Sir Arthur Wellesley)

1st Brigade (Major General Hill): 1st 5th Foot (944), 1st 9th Foot (761), 1st 38th Foot (953), a company 5th 60th Rifles.

2nd Brigade (Major General Ferguson): 36th Foot (591), 1st 40th Foot (923), 1st 71st Foot (935), a company 5th 60th Rifles.

3rd Brigade (Brigadier General Nightingall): 29th Foot (616), 1st 82nd Foot (904), a company 5th 60th Rifles.

4th Brigade (Brigadier General Bowes): 1st 6th Foot (943), 1st 32nd Foot (870), a company 5th 60th Rifles.

5th Brigade (Brigadier General C. Craufurd): 1st Battalion, 45th Foot (915), 91st Foot (917), a company 5th 60th Rifles.

6th or Light Brigade (Brigadier General Fane): 1st 50th Foot (945), 5th 60th Rifles (5 companies 604[1]), 2nd 95th Rifles (4 companies) (456).

7th Brigade (Brigadier General Anstruther): 2nd 9th Foot (633), 2nd 43rd Light Infantry (721), 2nd 52nd Light Infantry (8 companies) (654), 2nd 97th Foot (695).

8th Brigade (Brigadier General Acland): 2nd Foot (731) 20th Foot (7½ companies) (401), 1st 95th Rifles (2 companies) (200).

Cavalry: (Lieutenant Colonel Taylor): 20th Light Dragoons (240).

Artillery (Lieutenant Colonel Robe): 3 companies (226 men, 16 guns).

Portuguese (Colonel Trant): 6th Cavalry Regt (104), 11th Cavalry (50), 12th Cavalry (104), Lisbon Police Cavalry (41), 4th Artillery Regt (210), 12th Infantry (605), 21st Infantry (605), 24th Infantry (304), Porto Caçadores (562).

French Army

(Marshal Junot)

Delaborde's Division

1st Brigade (General of Brigade Montmorand): 3rd 2nd *Légère* (1,075), 3rd 4th *Légère* (1,098), 1st & 2nd 70th *Ligne* (2,358).

2nd Brigade (General of Brigade Thomières): 1st & 2nd 86th *Ligne* (1,945), 4th Swiss Regt (2 companies) (246).

Loison's Division

1st Brigade (General of Brigade Solignac): 3rd 12th *Ligne* (1,253), 3rd 15th *Légère* (1,305), 3rd 58th *Ligne* (1,428).

2nd Brigade (General of Brigade Charlot): 3rd 32nd *Ligne* (1,034), 3rd 82nd *Ligne* (963).

Reserve (General of Division Kellermann): 1st & 2nd 1st Provisional Grenadiers (1,050), 1st & 2nd 2nd Provisional Grenadiers (1,050).

Cavalry Division (General of Brigade Margaron): 1st Provisional (formerly 26th) *Chasseurs à Cheval* (263), 3rd Provisional Dragoons (640), 4th Provisional Dragoons (589), 5th Provisional Dragoons (659), Squadron Volunteer Cavalry (100).

Artillery: 4 batteries (375, 23 guns).

Appendix VIII

Modern Maps of the 1808 Battlefields

A modern map of the Óbidos battlefield. (*iGEO*)

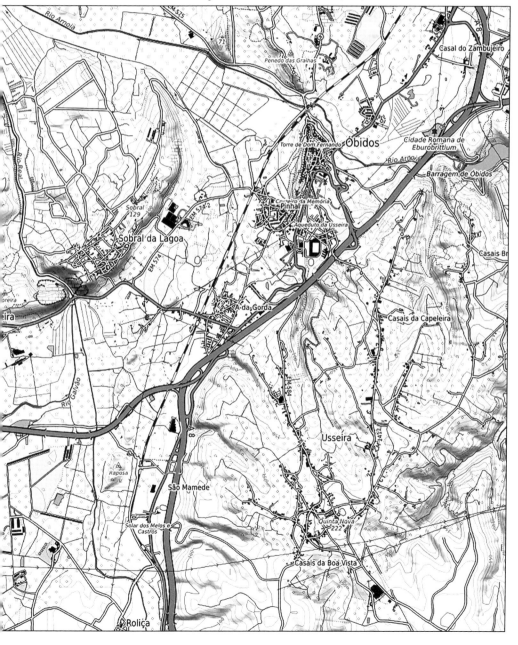

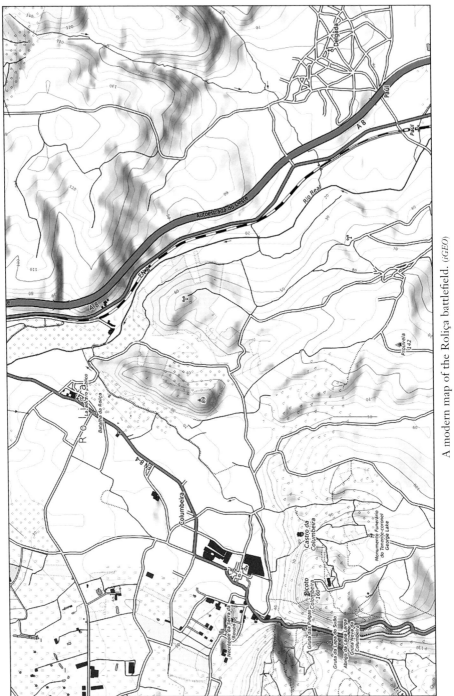

A modern map of the Roliça battlefield. (*iGEO*)

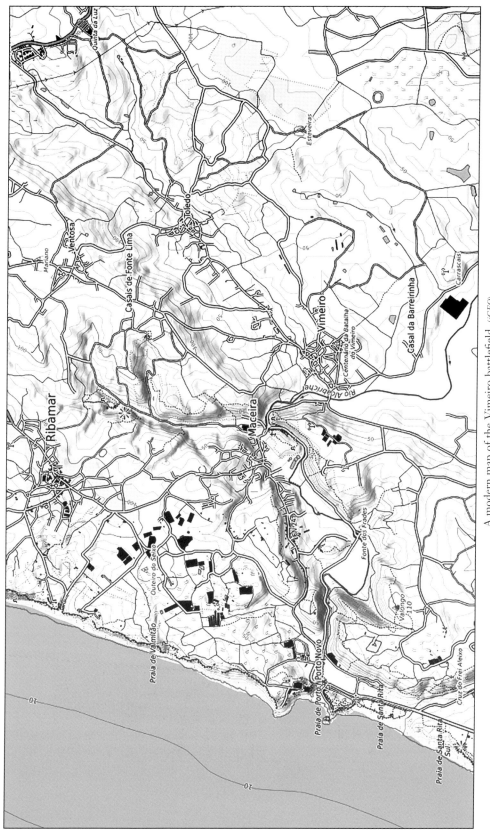

A modern map of the Vimeiro battlefield. *(fGEO)*

The arrival of the British in the Peninsular and the evacuation of Juno's corps from Portugal in Royal Navy ships was a grave insult to Napoleon's imperial and military dignity. He was bound to react strongly.

Notes

Chapter 1: The Peninsula 1807 and Early 1808

1. 'Filching sugar islands' was a phrase coined in Parliament by the Leader of the Opposition, Richard Sheridan.
2. Taking the navies of Denmark and Portugal into French control along with a construction programme of twenty-two ships at ports like Antwerp on the Scheldt was, in the aftermath of Trafalgar in 1805, a part of Napoleon's plan to challenge the Royal Navy's dominance. The emperor's intent had suffered a setback when the British seized fifteen sail of the line belonging to the Danish fleet at Copenhagen in the summer of 1807.
3. This was France's second invasion of Portugal, having previously supported the Spanish and 'imposed a burdensome capitulation on Portugal' in 1801.
4. Having had the Danish fleet slip through his fingers at Copenhagen, Napoleon did not want to lose the ten sail of the Portuguese navy.
5. General Maximilien Foy, *Junot's Invasion of Portugal 1807–1808* (published posthumously by Baudouin Frères, 1827).
6. Ibid.
7. As Napoleon was actively campaigning against the Austrians, most of these reinforcements were raw recruits who had been largely trained on the march.
8. Wellington, 2nd Duke, *Supplementary Dispatches, Correspondence and Memoranda of Field Marshal Duke of Wellington*, Vol. IV (John Murray, London, 1860).
9. Alison, Sir Archibald, quoted in *History of Europe from the Commencement of the French Revolution* (Blackwood & Son, London, 1833).
10. Gurwood, Lt Col, *The Dispatches of Field Marshal The Duke of Wellington*, Vol. 4 (John Murray, London, 1835).
11. Fortescue, J.W., *The History of the British Army*, Vol. 1 (Macmillan and Co. Limited, London, 1910).
12. *Dispatches*, Vol. IV.
13. Oman.
14. Now known as Forte de Santa Catarina in Figueira da Foz. The fort had originally been captured by students from Coimbra University.
15. In 1802 King George III, largely at the instigation of Admiral John Jervis, Earl of St Vincent, granted the Marines the 'Royal' prefix.

Chapter 2: The 1808 Campaign Begins

1. At the Cintra Inquiry Captain Malcolm described the naval problem of the landing: 'There is always a very great difficulty in landing on the coast of Portugal in those months, owing to the swell which causes a considerable surf upon the beach. At Mondego Bay there is a river, but at the mouth of the river there is a bar on which generally there is a very considerable surf. During the time that I was there, there were only four or five days that we could pass it without danger in common boats, but at the Mondego we got a large supply of boats of the country, schooners and larger boats, which facilitated the landing very much.'

2. Leach, *Rough Sketches of the Life of an Old Soldier* (Longman, London, 1831).
3. Fane's 6th Brigade was sometimes referred to as the 'Light Brigade', despite the 45th Foot not being 'light'.
4. Harris, Benjamin, *Recollections of Rifleman Harris (old 95th), with anecdotes of his officers and his comrades* (H. Hurst, London, 1848).
5. Patterson, Captain John, *The Adventures of Captain John Patterson* (T. & W. Boone, London, 1837).
6. Warre, William, ed. Edmond Warre, *Letters from the Peninsula 1808–1812* (Leonaur, Oakpast Ltd, 2019).
7. Muir states that Lord Burghersh, on joining Wellesley's staff, probably explained the government's motives in keeping command from Sir John Moore.
8. Wellington, 2nd Duke, *Supplementary Dispatches, Correspondence and Memoranda of Field Marshal Duke of Wellington*, Vol. VI (John Murray, London, 1860).
9. Landscheit and Gleig, I., *The Hussar: A German Cavalryman in British Service* (Colburn, London, 1837).
10. Norbert Landscheit served as a sergeant in the émigré York Hussars until its disbandment in 1802, whereupon he joined the 20th Light Dragoons, serving with them in South Africa and at Montevideo in 1807.
11. Ross-Lewin, Major, *With the 32nd in the Peninsula* (Hodges, Figgis & Co., Ltd, Dublin, 1834).
12. Napier, W.E.P., *History of the War in the Peninsula*, Vol. I, third edition (Constable, London, 1992).
13. *Dispatches, Correspondence and Memoranda of Field Marshal Duke of Wellington*, Vol. 4.
14. Foy, General Maximilien, *Junot's Invasion of Portugal 1807–1808* (Worley Publications, Tyne and Wear, 2000).
15. *Supplementary Dispatches*, Vol. VI.
16. Dundas, General Sir David, *Rules and Regulations for the Formations, Field-Exercise and Movements of His Majesty's Forces* (War Office, 1792).
17. Jennings, Louis, ed., *The Crocker Papers*, Vol. 1 (John Murray, London, 1884).

Chapter 3: The Affair at Óbidos

1. Landmann, Colonel, *Recollections of my Military Life* (N&M Press, Uckfield, Sussex).
2. At the Cintra Inquiry Wellesley summed up what was supplied by the Portuguese and captured from the French during the campaign as a whole. The core issue was bread. 'The country afforded us no provisions excepting beef and wine, and I believe that from the time I landed in Portugal to the time I quitted the army on the 20th of September, the troops only received biscuit from the ships. As I have stated in my narrative, a small quantity of bread was left behind by the French at Alcobaça, and a small quantity at Caldas, and besides this, after I had given up the command when the army arrived in the neighbourhood of Torres Vedras, a small quantity of flour was got, which had likewise been left behind by the French. While I commanded the army this bread supplied the consumption of the Portuguese troops, 1,650 in number, who were with me, and afterwards I believe that the Officers of the army received some baked bread from the Commissariat. But I am of the opinion that no exertion would have drawn from Portugal a supply of bread sufficient for that army.'
3. Francisco, de la Fuente, *Dom Miguel Pereira Forjaz: his early career and role in the Mobilization and Defence of Portugal during the Peninsular War, 1807–1814* (PhD thesis, Florida State University, 1980).
4. *Supplementary Dispatches*, Vol. VI.
5. The 1807 edition was translated into Portuguese for the Caçadores in 1810 by Captain William Warre.

6. Olferman, Captain Ernst, 97th Foot, *The Field Day* (The Royal Military Panorama, October 1813). Olferman had been a brigade major in the 4th, 7th and Light divisions.

7. The historian of the 60th notes, without clarifying the figure of seventeen missing, that 'in circumstances such as these some of the missing riflemen subsequently returned'.

8. Captain Pakenham was Wellesley's brother-in-law but, in his dispatch, he does not apportion blame to him or Travers.

Chapter 4: The Combat of Roliça

1. Landmann, Colonel, *Recollections of my Military Life* (N&M Press, Uckfield, Sussex).

2. Some have questioned Wellesley using the tower at the southern end of Óbidos on the basis that he could not see much. In fact, the army was already advancing from Caldas and Landmann had already observed the enemy from the same place as a part of his reconnaissance with Brigadier Fane. 'In the course of our rambles along the top of the Moorish walls, and while we were looking at the eastern hills through our telescopes, resting on the battlements … some of the inhabitants [of Óbidos] exclaimed that they could perceive the enemy, in their white canvas greatcoats and they appeared to be in considerable force, moving slowly on the skirt of a wood. At first sight I was convinced that the information was correct, and both the General and his Aide-de-Camp were of the same opinion; but, after I had carefully examined the supposed enemy with my famous three-foot telescope, by Watson! I clearly perceived that we had been deceived, for it turned out to be a large herd of goats, mostly white.' This was, of course, the same telescope used by Wellesley on Sunday, 17 August.

3. Leslie, Charles, *With the 29th Regiment in the Peninsula* (Leonaur, 2012).

4. Napier, William, *History of the War in the Peninsula* (Constable, London, 1992).

5. Foy, General Maximilien, *Junot's Invasion of Portugal 1807–1808* (Worley Publications, Tyne and Wear, 2000).

6. The companies Foy is referring to had been formed into four grenadier battalions and were at the time of the battle marching with General Junot from Lisbon.

7. Although there were several versions of older ammunition pouches still in service, by 1808 the standard pouch contained sixty rounds.

8. Patterson, Captain John, *The Adventures of Captain John Patterson* (T. & W. Boone, London, 1837).

9. Initially it would seem that the 29th briefly faced several companies of red-coated Swiss soldiers, who indicated that they wanted to surrender. Presumably the French quickly intervened.

10. *Supplementary Dispatches*, Vol. VI.

11. Lipscombe, Nick, *Wellington's Guns* (Osprey, Oxford, 2013).

12. Wood, George, *The Subaltern Officer* (Septimus Prowett, 1825).

13. Anon, *A Soldier of the Seventy-First* (Leo Cooper, London, 1975). Inside a copy of the book in the regimental library is a note from the editor that the story came from James Todd, not 'Thomas' or 'TS'.

14. British legislation prevented foreign corps serving in the UK, except on the Isle of Wight. Being made up of Germans and Swiss, for the 60th North Americans the isle was their natural home. The ban on serving in mainland Britain did not, however, extend to the KGL, being recruited from the King's Hanoverian territories.

15. *Supplementary Dispatches*, Vol. XIII, Appendices.

Chapter 5: Piquets and Preparations for Battle

1. Patterson, Captain John, *The Adventures of Captain John Patterson* (T. & W. Boone, London, 1837).

2. Foy, General Maximilien, *Junot's Invasion of Portugal 1807–1808* (Worley Publications, Tyne and Wear, 2000).
3. Landmann, Colonel, *Recollections of my Military Life* (N&M Press, Uckfield, Sussex).
4. Wood, George, *The Subaltern Officer* (Septimus Prowett, 1825).
5. *Dispatches*, Vol. IV. Letter to the Duke of York after Vimeiro.
6. *Dispatches*, Vol. IV.
7. The 52nd was incomplete: a brig with 200 men had yet to arrive, having fallen back from the convoy.
8. *Supplementary dispatches.*
9. At the Cintra Inquiry Burrard refuted the idea that he ever intended to hand command to another commander.
10. Harris's memory has again not served him well: the field officer in charge of the piquets that night was Major Hill of the 50th Regiment (see Patterson). Captain Charles Napier arrived later with Sir John Moore's force and gained his step to major much later in the campaign.
11. Harris, Benjamin, *Recollections of Rifleman Harris (old 95th), with anecdotes of his officers and his comrades* (H. Hurst, London, 1848).
12. Landscheit, Sergeant Norbert & G.R. Gleig, *The Hussar* (Leonaur Ltd, 2008).
13. Leach, *Rough Sketches of the Life of an Old Soldier* (Longman, London, 1831).

Chapter 6: Junot's Attacks on Vimeiro Hill

1. Warre, William, ed. Sir William Warre, *Letters from the Peninsula 1808–1812* (J. Murray, London, 1909).
2. Lipscombe, Nick, *Wellington's Guns* (Osprey, Oxford, 2013). The guns in each of the three batteries were probably two guns and a howitzer.
3. Anstruther, General Robert, *Note in Wyld's Atlas … 1808 to 1814* (London, 1841).
4. There is debate over whether this was a reverse slope position. There is some such ground in the area of the modern water tower but it is limited and could barely accommodate a single battalion let alone the deployment of two brigades. Note Captain Landmann's comment on page 98 and Anstruther's on page 100.
5. From various accounts it is clear that the British infantry were positioned on the reverse slope and would only have come forward as the French columns closed in.
6. Some have stated that Vimero Hill was not a reverse slope position. This is true in that it was not selected as such by Wellesley, but from certain angles, thanks to the slope and Vimeiro Hill's flat top, battalion commanders were able to make use of any reverse slope cover in their area, as so clearly described by Landmann. See photograph on p. 100.
7. Newbolt, Sir Henry, *Story of the Oxfordshire and Buckinghamshire Light Infantry* (N&M Press, Sussex, 2015).
8. Oblique marching was one step forward with the following thrown out 45 degrees to the left or right.
9. Lipscombe, Nick, *Wellington's Guns* (Osprey, Oxford, 2013).
10. Levine, Sir Augustus, *Historical Record of the Forty-Third Regiment – Monmouthshire Light Infantry* (Naval & Military Press, reprint of 1867 edition).
11. Hamilton, Sergeant Anthony, *Hamilton's Campaigns with Moore and Wellington* (Spellmount, 1988).

Chapter 7: The Attack on East Ridge and the Aftermath of Battle

1. Leslie, Charles, *With the 29th Regiment in the Peninsula* (Leonaur, 2012).
2. In what would become a hallmark of his style of command Wellesley, with matters under control around Vimeiro Hill, had ridden to the latest scene of action.
3. Anon, *A Soldier of the Seventy-First* (Leo Cooper, London, 1975).

4. Wood, George, *The Subaltern Officer* (Septimus Prowett, 1825).
5. Patterson, Captain John, *The Adventures of Captain John Patterson* (T. & W. Boone, London, 1837).
6. Colonel Torrens' evidence to the Cintra Inquiry, *Dispatches*, Vol. IV.
7. Inquiry into the Convention of Cintra, Royal College Chelsea, 14 November to 27 December 1808. During reports and questioning at the inquiry, all kinds of reasons for caution were advanced by Burrard as motives not to exploit Wellesley's victory at Vimeiro.
8. 4th battalions were normally depot battalions in France, but the need to feed troops to garrison and subdue the periphery of his empire meant that Napoleon needed to expand his regiments with often barely trained recruits.

Chapter 8: The Convention of Cintra and the French Evacuation

1. Foy, General Maximilien, *Junot's Invasion of Portugal 1807–1808* (Worley Publications, Tyne and Wear, 2000).
2. General Dalrymple as Governor of Gibraltar was 'our man' in the Peninsula in 1808 and was well placed to follow developments and Spanish politics. He was regarded as having done a good job in that sphere.
3. *Supplementary Dispatches*, Vol. VI.
4. Dalrymple, *Memoir written by General Sir Hew Dalrymple of his Proceedings ... at the commencement of the Peninsular War* (Thomas William Boone, London, 1830).
5. 'Cintra' is a misnomer. Dalrymple noted: 'A name improperly and unluckily applied to this treaty, as it produced an opinion that it *was* actually negotiated and concluded in that village, in a certain hall, in the Marialva Palace, whereas Cintra was in rear of the "formidable position", the possession of which was obtained by the Convention.'
6. *Supplementary Dispatches*, Vol. VI.
7. *The Times*, 19 September 1808.
8. Patterson, Captain John, *The Adventures of Captain John Patterson* (T. & W. Boone, London, 1837).
9. See also evidence on the difficulty of attacking entrenched positions in the country between Torres Vedras and Lisbon given during the Cintra Inquiry. *Dispatches*, Vol. IV.
10. Ross-Lewin, Major Harry, *With the Thirty-Second in the Peninsula* (Hodges, Figgis & Co. Ltd, London, 1854).
11. *Supplementary Dispatches*, Vol. XIII, Appendices.
12. The French garrison of Elvas was not finally evacuated until early October thanks to negotiating the end of the siege and the distance from Lisbon.
13. 15 July 1808, Viscount Castlereagh, Secretary of State, to Lieut. General Sir Hew Dalrymple. *Dispatches*, Vol. IV.
14. *Supplementary Dispatches*, Vol. XIII, Appendices.
15. Such were the vagaries of the dissemination of orders that some received the instruction to cut hair much earlier while on board ship en route to the Peninsula.
16. Dobbs, Captain John, *Recollections of an Old 52nd Man* (Spellmount, Staplehurst, 2000).
17. Ross-Lewin, Major, *With the Thirty-Second in the Peninsula* (Hodges, Figgis & Co. Ltd, London, 1854).
18. Landmann, Colonel, *Recollections of my Military Life* (N&M Press, Uckfield, Sussex).

Chapter 9: Portugal between the 1808 and 1809 Campaigns

1. The need for production of itineraries of route led to the formation of the Corps of Guides under Major Scrovell the following year. See Saunders, *The Talavera Campaign 1809* (Pen & Sword, Barnsley, 2023).

2. Castlereagh's dispatch of 25 September 1808.

3. During the Cintra Inquiry Wellesley answered a question on supply thus: 'The country afforded us no provisions excepting beef and wine, and I believe that from the time I landed in Portugal to the time I quitted the army on the 20th of September, the troops only received biscuit from the ships.'

4. Of Sir John's problems, Oman observed that 'In later years Wellington gradually succeeded in collecting a large and invaluable army of Spanish and Portuguese employees, who – in their own fashion – were as good campaigners as his soldiery, and served him with exemplary fidelity even when their pay was many months in arrears. But in 1808 this body of trained camp-followers did not exist, and Moore had the greatest difficulty in scraping together the transport that took him forward to Salamanca. As to commissariat arrangements, he found that even though he divided his army into several small columns and utilized as many separate routes as possible, it was not easy for the troops to live.' These commodities in a locality, however, ran out if the army was stationary for more than a couple of days.

5. Leslie, Charles, *With the 29th Regiment in the Peninsula* (Leonaur, 2012).

6. Sir Robert Wilson was rewarded with promotion to colonel and a knighthood, but fell out with Castlereagh and served with the Russian army before being reinstated and promoted to general rank.

7. Napier, George, *Passages in the Early Military Life of General George T. Napier, KCB* (London, 1884).

8. Leach, *Rough Sketches of the Life of an Old Soldier* (Longman, London, 1831). Ague was a catch-all term, but is generally a malarial or another illness involving fever and shivering.

9. Anon, *A Memoir of the Duke of Wellington*, Vol. IV (A. Fullerton and Co., London, 1814).

Appendix I: Lieutenant General Wellesley's orders for the Peninsular Expedition

1. Gurwood, *Dispatches*, Vol. IV.

2. Of this battalion Wellesley wrote to General Hill: 'The Veteran battalion must be put out of the question, as that corps must go into the garrison of Gibraltar.' (*Dispatches*, Vol. IV.)

Appendix V: The Convention of Cintra

1. Wellington, Second Duke of, *Supplementary Dispatches*, Vol. XIII, *Appendix 1794–1812* (John Murray, Albemarle Street, London, 1871).

Appendix VI: On the March

1. Blakeney, Robert, ed. J. Sturgis, *A Boy in the Peninsular War* (John Murray, London, 1899).

2. Patterson, Captain John, *The Adventures of Captain John Patterson* (T. & W. Boone, London, 1837).

Appendix VII: Order of Battle – Vimeiro

1. Total for the battalion and its detachments to other brigades.

Index